Playing in the Sandbox

A Leader's Guide to Moving Their Team
Through the Good, Bad and Ugly of
Cubicle Nation

By Tammy Redmon

Creative Force Press

Creative Force Press

Playing in the Sandbox
© 2013 by Tammy Redmon
www.theteamoptimizer.com

This title is also available as an eBook. Visit
www.CreativeForcePress.com/titles for more information.

Published by Creative Force Press
4704 Pacific Ave, Suite C, Lacey, WA 98503
www.CreativeForcePress.com

Cover design by www.ZenDezignz.com

ISBN: 978-1-939989-05-5

Printed in the United States of America

DEDICATION

To Grandpa Archie and Grandpa Don

It wasn't until your passing that I realized the full extent of what you taught me growing up. Through your servant's hearts, I learned the value of community, the honor of serving others, the love of family, the joy of trying something new, and always having a playful spirit.

You will forever be in my heart.

TABLE OF CONTENTS

PREFACE

I distinctively remember the day I knew it was time to leave *'cubicle nation.'* It was a spring afternoon, and I had just received a phone call from the Governor with explicit instructions to stop the project I had been working on or he would *find me a new opportunity elsewhere.*

It didn't take much for this state employee to realize that *"new opportunity elsewhere"* did not mean promotion. Siberia, perhaps?

While that day 12 years ago still makes me smile, it was a wake-up call that I carry with me forever. It taught me that while I may be excelling in my position on a team, I can still have a perpetual bruise on my forehead from running into the same brick walls. It was the catalyst moment that propelled me from a demoralized member of a team to taking responsibility for my professional happiness.

Of course, that wasn't the first time I had heard such a sentiment about the quality of my work. Just six months prior to that call from the Governor, my office received a phone call from a certain Senator who told me, "I don't care how much your projects *really* cost, just make them look cheap."

During that season of disillusion, being pulled back and feeling suppressed, I learned that while some on your team may have a *service with excellence* mindset, others, even your boss, may not. If I was feeling held back or restrained from truly excelling in my current position, it was up to me to do something about it. So, I decided to pack up my successes and leave a career that I was passionate about to help other teams and leaders who also felt held back, broke, busted and disgusted with their jobs find joy once again.

Truth-be-told, it was those two distinct, abhorring moments in my career that I am most thankful for today.

If it were not for those experiences, which uprooted my comfort and tested my character, I don't believe I would be doing the work with teams and leaders that I do around the world today. It took a major shift in my perspective regarding the potential impact I could make in a career that I truly enjoyed to move me away from that proverbial brick wall called *limiting beliefs* and *unmet expectations*.

Throughout my career, I have always maintained the attitude of work as service. I learned that at a very young age from my grandfathers; two men whom I so admired growing up, who fought for our country and served their community with honor. Through them, I saw the high value of serving others. Today, I serve at the pleasure of my clients.

When I was in *cubicle nation*, I served at the pleasure of my boss, director and yes, even the Governor. However, not all of my work brought a sense of pleasure to those around me. Why not?

Because as someone who works to serve with excellence, I quickly discovered the pain of working in an environment of mediocrity.

What I learned about myself that fateful year was that I had been avoiding looking at the writing on the wall for several previous years. The negative messages that I received from the team that I was working with were always loud and most often clear, but as an eternal optimist, I rejected them as false. Having been told by my boss to stop bringing ideas to her because they created more work for everyone should have sent me immediately running for greener pastures. But, I was not a quitter. Why should I give up because of the lack of someone else's ability to see opportunity? No, I kept pressing in.

Like many of the people I work with today who feel they are part of a dysfunctional team, I wasn't going to allow the naysayers to put me down or hold me back from serving with excellence. And yet, hold me back is exactly what happened over time.

As I persevered through growing my knowledge bank account and expanding my sphere of influence in my community, the day came when a decision had to be made: either I was going to adopt the mindset of the environment I was working within or I was going to break free of it. For some time, I just pushed to *get better* at my J.O.B.

and ignored the people around me. I became a silo of one. It wasn't long before I realized that people didn't *want* to work with me. They couldn't relate to who I had become, and even I started to not recognize myself in the mirror.

Feeling oppressed in that environment by an attitude of *'just get by'* and *'because we've always done it this way'* was killing me on the inside. My heart was no longer in the game, because my autonomy was cut off at the knees. Eventually my spirit was nearly broken, and I no longer loved the work.

I hadn't sunk to the depths of an underperformer, but I had given up on my ability to make a difference. No longer was I a good servant to the mission and vision of the organization. The writing was on the wall; I just needed to read it and take action.

All of the degrees and certifications I attained were my way of seeking to be more excellent, and yet none of them impacted my ability to be successful in that environment. The other members of my team had made up their minds to reject what I put forward.

Was it because I scared them?
Was it because I pushed too hard?
Was it because I failed to partner with them?

Perhaps all three. Or maybe it was simply a blessing in disguise meant to propel me into a career that I truly adore, giving me the chance to make an impact on a much larger scale.

Not all failure is bad. And defeat is powerful.

> *"Far better is it to dare mighty things,*
> *to win glorious triumphs,*
> *even though checkered by failure...*
> *than to rank with those poor spirits*
> *who neither enjoy nor suffer much,*
> *because they live in a gray twilight*
> *that knows not victory nor defeat."*
> – Theodore Roosevelt

Planning My Exit Strategy

Taking my inner defeat in hand, I made the decision to leave my position. Interestingly, it was at a time when the leadership regime was making a major transition. And for anyone who knows a thing or two about government, regime change can be really great...or not so much. However, I found myself being courted to stay. A carrot was dangled in front of me; a nice, shiny carrot tempting me with a new, greater opportunity. But, it wasn't enough this time.

I was not motivated by the prize of the potential challenge, because I had lost my heart for the whole lot. I knew enough about culture in organizations to know that when you lose your heart, it's time to go.

When your team members reach their expiration

date, it is best to let them go quietly versus trying to extend their shelf life.

I left with my awards in hand and my dignity in tow. And I have never looked back.

You may be wondering why I chose to become an expert on teams. You may be asking how I leaped from there to here. The transition was actually rather easy, but I had to first discover my compelling 'why,' and then be relentless about modeling it to the world.

With a background in intercultural communications and organizational development, I further pursued deepening my knowledge bank in organizational psychology and got certified as an executive coach. Yes, I amassed more paper for my walls, though it all sat quietly in boxes. I use the knowledge today, but the best education came from the experience of refusing to feel stuck or demoralized by the work environment I had once succeeded in.

When my purpose became clear, my 'why' became the driving force behind me. Today I have the distinct pleasure of helping leaders who are frustrated with their dysfunctional teams, take the groups they have and transform them into the teams they want.

For the past decade, I have collected story after story from people who were much like me; people who wanted to make a difference with their work but felt confined by the silo they were placed within. I have created a tapestry of humanity in the workplace with each thread of influence left behind in my work. My heart is to see people take a stand for their passion at work and be more than they ever thought possible. My mission is to expose the power of possibility in teams and leaders by allowing truth-telling and revealing the soul within.

To get my transformative work out to as many teams and leaders as possible is the goal for writing this book. Try as I might, it's not physically possible to personally coach all who need help, but my hope is that this book wakes the evangelist within everyone who reads it. Take a stand for excellence and rebuke the mindset of mediocrity in the workplace!

Get Ready! Get Ready! Get Ready!
Your journey is just a page turn away!

INTRODUCTION

On a typical, rainy, Pacific Northwest day, I stood quietly listening to my Governor say these words to me, "*Stop what you are doing or you will be moved into a new opportunity.*"

While my ears rang with that warning signal, the breaking of my spirit was a far louder cry. Never before during my career had I ever felt such rejection for simply doing my job with excellence. I was confident I was a good steward with the resources I managed and I faithfully served my team with joy.

At that moment, I realized that simply serving and good stewardship wasn't enough. It did not matter that I discovered a gaping hole in my agency's budget, which had been leaking money out like a faucet left on for decades. *Why was it an unwelcome discovery?* I couldn't understand the reaction from my leaders.

I, like many of you, had just become a demoralized team member in "*cubicle nation.*"

If there was a change to be made, it was up to me to make it. I was taking back my pride and personal power. I began by breaking down the walls that confined me in a job where my talent, passion and expertise – not to mention my good stewarding – were no longer welcome.

Since that experience 12 years ago, I have a new, single-minded mission: to help the weary employee trapped in a *"because we've always done it this way"* workplace mentality; to teach them how to break free of mediocrity, and to change attitudes hindering them from getting their heart's desire.

When I work with teams around the world, I like to call it *Playing in the Sandbox.* It is a metaphor that seems to be universal; everyone understands it. *Playing in the Sandbox* evokes a picture in our minds that takes us back to a time and place when we co-created fantastic structures and first learned the power of negotiation, team-building and sharing.

Yet in today's workplace, those same skills we gained in the neighborhood sandbox are often abandoned for a *'just get by'* and *'keep it to yourself'* way of co-existing.

Today's leaders are frustrated with the lack of interest from their teams. They are spinning in circles, managing the underperformer on the team who can build the necessary *widget*, but end up costing one-third of the leader's time in clean-up mode. Meanwhile, other team members feel besieged with the extra work on their desks because of the one cog in the wheel not pulling their weight. And to top it off, they have a leader who consistently focuses on what's *not* working instead of promoting what is.

So where did the rules of the sandbox go? What happened to co-creating fantasy with ease, using a shovel and a bucket? Why did we abandon the negotiation skills we used to succeed on the playground at 5 years old only to pick up vile attitudes and apathetic work habits as adults?

To quote a line from a great film, *Cool Hand Luke,* **'What we've got here is a failure to communicate."** A young Paul Newman, portraying a prisoner in chains, was bound by the rules and wanted to break free. While creating the life he truly wanted, his rebel spirit took the whole team down. And the prison captain was hell-bent on making sure he made an example out of the one with the spirit of rebellion.

Now, in today's world of work, the chains have become paychecks and the rebellion has been replaced with indifference. Both are destructive, tearing at the fabric of our souls and deteriorating the hope in our hearts. **What we've got here is a failure to communicate.** Sadly, the one who is causing the dissension is only spoken about at the water cooler or in the parking lot, when what is needed is a bold conversation in the boardroom.

This book is about to change that.

Over the next twelve chapters we will dive deep into the mindset and beliefs that are attacking our teams today. Together, we will deconstruct the habits and attitudes that are fostering the dysfunction as we draft a compelling 'why' for change. And you will begin to develop the strength and stamina for starting necessary, bold conversations of your own. You will become mission-driven to promote a healthy team environment.

In the first four chapters, we will deconstruct the team, while revisiting and redefining some of the rules of the sandbox. *There will be little to do with data and popular research statistics. I need to be clear about that: I am not giving you statistics.* I am speaking to you from my personal experience; offering powerful tools to help you be your best self at work; to change your whole life and make it completely satisfying. It is what I am *living*, and want you to live, too.

This book is also filled with stories of leaders and team members much like you and me; catalysts for transformation who have braved the winds of change.

My vision for this book is to have it be a tool guide, a resource for teams and leaders to use on a daily basis. *Playing in the Sandbox* can be that special tool used again and again in support of transforming the way you work with the people around you. We spend more time at work than we do at home, so why not make it time well spent! At the end of each chapter are powerful questions to ask during conflicts and situations when good communication is needed.

After we demystify teams and re-engage with the

rules of the sandbox, we will spend chapters five through seven on establishing the culture of a healthy team. It has much to do with the responsibility you and I have as individuals to both the success and/or failure of teams. There is no escaping or hiding. If you have heard it once, you have heard it a hundred times:

"The tide raises all ships in the harbor."

That means for the team to change, every single person on the team must take an honest look in the mirror and ask, "What is *my* role here to move *us* forward?"

I will never forget the day I looked at an elected official, who was completely blind to his personal impact on the team and how he negatively affected people, and told him, *"Like it or not, you became a leader of people when you had the guts to put your name on the ballot."*

See, he was in a position for other reasons; reasons that didn't include supporting the people he managed or helping them be successful. This official resented me telling him that he *was* a leader and it was time to step up and lead the people!

Yes, this elected official really did not see himself as a leader! The staff people he worked with were going to be in that job far beyond his stop along the political byway, and they deserved to be led, not patted on the head and pacified. His utter breakdown in front of me was revealing on many levels. It opened my eyes to the notion that when we take on a position without a vision for how we partner with others, it keeps our vessels tied to the shore where the tide has no impact for raising us up *together*.

You will learn more about the journey of this former politician in chapter seven. It is one of my greatest accomplishments, and saddest experiences, as a team coach. Throughout chapters eight, nine and ten, we will begin to construct a strategy for *designing* (emphasis on 'designing') a healthy team. Yes, even you, the one who may have no ambition of leading a team, will learn how each of us has a natural leadership style, and how we can all lend our expertise to designing the perfect team that we want to play with for years to come.

You will learn the 5 P's of a team and how to apply them with every decision you make. Again, let me encourage you: *Playing in the Sandbox* is not just for people who manage or lead others. It *is* for the whole team. Every member of your team will find this resource useful for their collective success. So, if you have found yourself resisting (like my friend, the former politician) leading others, my invitation for you now is to declare that you *are* a leader, and people are waiting for you to step up and lead. Lead, even if it is simply leading *yourself* to high performance.

One of my favorite conversations to have with clients is the one that promotes the discovery of the underperformer on the team, or the under-performance factors of a team. The reason I love this part of my work is because it lights the brightest fire of change. I have found that managers today get so caught up in *over*-compensating for *under*performance, they are often left feeling depleted and disjointed, becoming immune to the core of the issue. So, in the middle of the book, we will talk about how to identify this problem and how to build an action plan to change it.

I have been told that this part of my work is where the secret weapon of every team emerges. From my perspective, I think it's simple: show a team how to use the tools they already have within their toolbox for success. It can be the easy switch from using a hammer, when a Philips-head screwdriver is all that's needed.

By the time we get to chapters eleven and twelve, you will be well on your way to mastering the *team* concept. You will have a greater understanding of roles and responsibilities and new tactical skills to manage any conversation. In these final two chapters, we are going to discuss the deeper topics of *Ceiling of Complexity and Capacity*. Both have to do with the systems we put in place to propel us forward or limit our growth, but neither one has an easy solution to uproot the depth of the problem. However, from my years of working at building systems with teams, streamlining the ones they already have, and getting companies off the round-a-bout and into the performance lane, the pain of change gives a great return on the bottom line.

I can't say it gives the *greatest* return, because opening up the dialogue with our people to uncover attitudes and expectations is what's most transforming. But, I can say that to really grow to the heights where leaders want their teams cannot happen without diving into the complexity of the team and their capacity.

We will round out the book with a resources section that includes seven suggestions for asking *powerful questions* and some of my favorite *bold conversation starters* for those times when you just need to *get real*.

So, in preparation for your journey through the *Sandbox*, here are some thoughts for you to consider:

On a scale of 1 (low) to 10 (high), how satisfied are you with your present role on the team? (If you picked 5, take a longer look in the mirror)

What if nothing changes in your current situation? How will that impact your future performance?

What causes you the greatest pain, right now, in your team?

What resources do you have available to change those dynamics?

What is your compelling 'why' for doing the work you do? And how long do you suppose that will sustain you?

When you think about the challenges you face daily, what or who is the cause of them? (Double check where the finger is pointing)

If you could have a do-over in life, and could be or do anything you want, what would you be or do? What's stopping you from going after it now?

My hope for you, after reading this book, will be that you find a sense of purpose again. Or, if you have your purpose, you find the audacity to walk it out boldly and lead yourself and your people to their mountain-top experience.

Welcome to the *Sandbox*. It's going to be a fantastic ride!

1

THE CASE FOR YOUR DEMORALIZED TEAM

"All meaningful and lasting change starts on the inside and works its way out." –Lou Tice

Over the years, I have seen many teams move from underperformance to excelling and hitting the targets and measures set before them. While I wish I could say the transformation was done in just a few easy steps or without hardship, you wouldn't believe me, even if I wrote that here.

The truth is, moving teams forward – teams entrenched in fear because they don't trust one another or their leader – takes serious work.

It takes stamina.
It takes commitment.
It takes breaking down the barriers of fear and addressing the core issues that are prevalent in the culture.

Transforming your team requires a commitment to looking deep within each individual and the collective culture they co-create to promote change. Any factors that impede forward progress must be exposed. It may seem that a demoralized team would be obvious to identify. As clear as we think it should be, it can actually be quite tricky. Why? *Because people have become really good at avoiding truth-telling in the office.* They become focused on self-preservation and even self-promotion, versus focusing on the results for the whole system's success.

But, before we can address the issues or even symptoms, we need to talk about the feelings that lead to the decisions every member of your team makes. What is the demoralized team member (who lacks autonomy and drive) feeling? What exactly *is* a demoralized team member? Let's start with the definition of the root word itself.

Demoralize:
1. to deprive (a person or persons) of spirit, courage, discipline, etc.; destroy the morale of: The continuous barrage demoralized the infantry.
2. to throw (a person) into disorder or confusion; bewilder: We were so demoralized by that one wrong turn that we were lost for hours.
3. to corrupt or undermine the morals of.
(Source - dictionary.com)

At this very moment, I can hear the collective rejection of that word associated with your team. You may not understand or even see these characteristics as an active expression among your team, and that could be part of the problem. Often, leaders build blind spots to the very issues that have the greatest impact against their success. And your team may also not be able to verbalize their feeling of being demoralized. It probably shows up a little differently for each person, but at the core, they all feel deprived of being able to put forth their best self at work.

Look around your office. Examine for a moment the personalities, success factors and fail points of your team. Begin to ask what propels the behavior that you see. Spend time here, even if it's uncomfortable to do so. The time you invest in understanding the members of your team is time well spent in the long run.

As Dan Pink so eloquently breaks down for us in his best-selling book, *Drive*, every person on your team wants, and needs at a core level, to feel they are making a difference. They are no longer motivated by the carrot and stick: the almighty paycheck. What motivates our people to move the proverbial needle forward day in and day out is the ability to have autonomy at work. They are driven by a heart-centered purpose and motivated by making a difference first.

Every member of the team wants to know when they show up at work, the effort they put forth is contributing to a greater good. It's the job of every leader to ensure that their teams know, hear and believe they make a difference.

In the early years of my professional career, I realized over time that the work I contributed was not feeding my soul. It was not having the impact that I hoped it would, and it had absolutely nothing to do with the quality or quantity of my work. It had everything to do with the values that I held deep inside of me, at my core, and how they were in direct opposition to the values of my leaders.

This type of disconnect among leaders and the members of their team is one of the deepest issues to uproot in every organization. It is often, also, the most painful. Getting to the root requires a big shovel, digging deep into the soil of the workplace to begin cultivating change.

Leaders – so how do you know if you have a demoralized team on your hands?

First, you may notice that I refer to the whole team in that last question. The reason is that if you have one feeling demoralized, they're all feeling less than their best working under your leadership. From my experience and observation, I would nearly always be correct in making the bold claim that having a demoralized team member is a "one-size fits all" scenario, to some degree.

If we could put a recorder in the break room or

parking lot at your office, we might hear some of the following comments from your team. These are actual comments from members of teams I have coached:

"Everything I try to do just keeps getting pushed back on my desk. I can't seem to do anything to please her."

"I receive little direction on how to get my project moving. He expects me to know what he wants without telling me directly."

"Did you see who just got a promotion? I can't believe they picked him, we keep fixing his mistakes and he gets the pay raise. It doesn't seem like anyone around here cares about the work."

"I am just going to sit here with my head down because I will outlast the director anyway. Why try to do it his way, he's just here for a notch in his belt. I've outlasted the last three; he is no different."

"If it's going to get done, it's up to me to do it."

Now let me be clear. We are *not* talking about office gossip or disgruntled employees. These are members of every team in America who come to work each day wondering what twists and turns will come their way. They work for leaders who know little about leading people and are prompted by moving work through at a high velocity. However, the work won't move if the people aren't empowered to move it.

The notion that our people are paid to do a job and should just do it without question is ancient thinking. It's a dangerous mindset still prevalent in today's workplace. Every person who shared those comments with me believed in their heart that they could not change their environment and had become victims to the disorder and confusion that was rampant in the office.

Victim...should be a four-letter word. Victim mentality in the workplace is actually (in my humble opinion) the most insidious disease impacting our performance and capacity as humans today.

When we address the mindset of our people, at every level, we will impact change. If we avoid understanding how people perceive one another and the work, growth will remain stagnant. We will fail.

Every healthy leader I talk with wants a team built of achievement-oriented employees. But often the reward of compensation is what's tied to the desired result or specific outcome. Relying on this to motivate our team is problematic, because it assumes that our team is motivated by the almighty dollar as a *sole* driver for behavior and performance. Interestingly, it also creates an apathetic workplace. Why? Because those folks who aren't hitting the numbers often don't really believe they ever can, causing them to adopt for the *head down, just get by* daily way of operating. Again, claiming victim status.

There are employees everywhere that wear their victim hat like a red badge of courage, or in some cases, a scarlet letter. They may appear as feeling demoralized, but that is just a coat with different stripes. Please do not confuse the two. A demoralized team member is often one of your greatest producers on the team. But, if not taken care of, they will leave for opportunity elsewhere.

A victim on the team, however, is someone you need to examine closely to evaluate the overall cost to the team that their attitude or their performance costs. Is their part weighted the same as every other member of your team? If *no* is your answer, then you might apply my golden rule: slow to hire – quick to fire. I encourage you to be bold!

When you take a broad look at your team, you will see the folks who are fighting to make things different. They may even be the ones that frustrate you the *most*. And you will see the ones that are simply just getting by and busily pointing fingers. It is imperative that you know the difference between *victim* and *demoralized* because the way to approach them is starkly different.

Just to help build the case for resolving the demoralized and dissolving the victim, let's take a look at the victim.

A victim is someone who believes, sincerely, that

they are the center of some personal conspiracy; that the world and everyone in it are against all their endeavors. Ironically, it is this belief that results in the endless gathering of evidence by the victim to prove this is true. And so, it is often difficult for the victim to see the truth through this clouded paradigm of self-deceit and defeat.

The 10 Signs of a Victim Mentality:

1. Failure to Accept Responsibility
This person will do anything to absolve him/herself from personal responsibility for any aspect of their lives. This results in the next symptom – blaming.

2. The Serial Blamer
This person absolves themselves from responsibility by apportioning blame to any other party, other than themselves. They usually develop the following skill.

3. Rationalization
The victim is adept at drawing creatively from circumstance to apportion blame to external factors. They use all their creative energies to construct a perfect prison for themselves. This construct results in the next symptom.

4. Feeling Helpless
If you say something often enough, you start to believe it, and victims start believing fairytales their minds have designed to keep them safe from their own accountability. This results in extreme feelings of helplessness and isolation. The next symptom is a

natural follow-up.

5. Self-Pity
Victims often feel sorry for themselves. This is a vicious cycle where the serial blamer and rationalizer begin to feel more self–pity. The cycle continues, creating more antagonistic forces that seemingly strip personal choice away. They often resort to:

6. Living in the Past
A failure to accept responsibility means a failure to accept things as they are in the present. This person will then either seek solace in the past, where things were "simpler," or again, resort to blaming the past for the current state of their environment. They tend to:

7. Focus on the Problems
They occupy themselves with problems and are often the people who complain any chance they get. Victims love attention and validation, relishing any opportunity to complain about their problems. During this whine fest they often say:

8. If Only/What If
This is a sure sign of a victim mentality! They do not accept things as they are, and they wear regrets like a crucifix. Then, the cycle continues by:

9. Condemning Themselves
Woe is me, I am useless, there are too many forces against me, if only things were easier, just like in the good old days...This is a summation of a victim's

thought pattern, cleverly disguised by the rationalizer and the blamer.

10. Separation of Self

Victims separate themselves from anything that resembles responsibility, and as such, they are separate from the solution. They are as good at playing the waiting game as they are at playing the blame game.

But what if the leader is the one with the victim way of viewing the world? How can a team operate within *that* scenario? Sadly, many leaders do not see the impact their day to day actions have on their team or how their way of speaking to a problem or an opportunity sets the tone for the entire group. That can leave any number of people feeling unable to impact change or be successful at work.

Leaders, *you* have the single greatest ability to change the culture, mindset and success factors for your team. Yes, you! But first, examine yourself in the mirror to get a better glimpse of what actions you might be doing that cause your team to withdraw.

A great solution here is to get a board of advisors, trusted truth-tellers around you to reflect what they see you doing. These are people who *don't* work for you. If you only listen to the people on your payroll, you will never get the full reflection of your behaviors that are potentially sabotaging your team. Now, that doesn't mean you don't want feedback from your team, because it's important you take it. What it does mean is that an outsider's perspective into the problems you are facing is needed to get a fresh approach, an open-minded look into the 'why' you and your team are performing the way you are. When you hold a person's paycheck, they may feel the need to withhold the whole truth if it's ugly.

If you want to be really bold, ask my favorite member of every team for their feedback: the *newest* member. If the latest addition to the team has been there less than 6 months, they are always the *first* person on the team that I want to talk with when I start coaching for breakthrough. Why, you ask? Because they don't yet have the rose colored glasses and they see every crack in your sidewalk.

Yes, you read that correctly. The newest member of your team has the freshest perspective—that (most) people tend to reject. Why is their opinion discounted? *"Because he/she hasn't been here long enough or put in his time here yet."* And when we genuinely sit with them to explore the view from their chair, they often give the golden ticket right up front. They can spot who the victim is and where the root of the demoralization is stemming from.

The caveat to this conversation is safety. A leader's job is to create a safe environment for the 'newbie' to share their insights. A neutral, third party person could come in to help put them at ease.

Now, please, before you go soliciting feedback from the newest member of your team, first be completely open and ready to receive it. There can be no personal attachment to the outcome other than to hear a fresh perspective.

Be prepared. The feedback might be a bit uncomfortable, and any cloudiness or blind spots you unknowingly have will show up. If you can't say, beyond the shadow of a doubt, that you're ready for the feedback, don't ask the questions.

So...now what?

It's time to ask some powerful questions of yourself. It's time to take inventory. Whether you're the leader of the team or a team member, all change happens when we examine our inner self first.

Questions to Ask Yourself

How do I fit on my team?

Where do I see myself on the team?

On a scale of 1 (low) to 10 (high) what is my ability to impact change?

Questions to Ask About Your Team

What do I see on my team? (strengths, weakness, opportunities, threats)

Who is the highest performer on the team and why?

Who is the lowest performer on the team and why?

On a scale of 1 (low) to 10 (high) how is the morale on the team?

If one thing could change for our team to move forward, what would it be?

Finish the Following Sentence:

If I am being totally honest about my team, I would say they....

2

THE SANDBOX AND YOUR TEAM

"To up-level performance, start by decreasing wheel spin and increasing creative flow."
–Tammy Redmon

Not all shovels are created equal. At least that is what I learned in the neighborhood sandbox as a child. Our sandbox was the one place where all the kids wanted to come hangout, create and play. We learned the rules of engagement very early on. Everyone understood that to be invited into the sandbox, they had to adhere to the agreed-upon rules or they would not be welcome for long. The rules were, in fact, pretty simple to follow as 5-year-olds. It was only when the big kids came into the box that things got messy, or if someone came with a bad attitude that day.

In today's cubicle nation, things aren't much different. You have teams that work very well together because they all understand the ground rules of engagement. You also have teams that, by adding one or two new members, get thrown into chaos and disarray. And of course, we know there are no guarantees everyone will show up day in and day out with the same *let's get it done together* attitude.

On your team, every member comes into work with a different set of tools; different shovels, so to speak. They approach with their familiar set of tools, and then see the assortment of new tools already there. You, as the leader, can give them instructions, define the ways we work together and set up the targets and measures. But, depending on what each member comes in with, it can affect the outcome for the team. So, you must learn to adapt quickly to the changes, attitudes and even rebellion so the team can accomplish the task at hand together. Together is key, because we aren't building fiefdoms: we are moving the needle forward, toward the common goal.

For the past two years, I have asked the same question at every speaking event. Each time I ask, I get the same response from the audience. My question is:

"What were the rules of the sandbox?"

Rule #1 - Don't Throw Sand
Rule #2 - Don't Take Another Person's Shovel
Rule #3 - Don't Knock Over Someone's Castle

Rule #4 - Share Your Tools

And what's the one odd response I received that still makes me giggle today?

Honorary Rule #5 – Don't Eat the Sand...because the neighborhood cat uses it as a litter box!

Each of the sandbox rules we adhered to as kids apply today in cubicle nation. It seems we have set them aside as adults and commonly break every one of them with ease. But, when followed, the rules work. They are not a respecter of persons or discriminator of age.

Let's break it down one step further. If playing in the sandbox required being a rule-follower to be part of the community, how is it we set the same rules aside as adults without a second thought? Why do so many team members today ignore the ground rules of a high-performing team? I am not talking here about the creative people that press boundaries or think outside the box. Of course, we celebrate those people as high achievers and top performers. I *am* talking about the folks who purposefully set aside the harmonious sandbox rules in what appears to be an act of self-sabotage. But it ends up causing something else altogether: chaos and frustration.

Take a look at those four simple rules; they set the boundaries for the power of negotiating and getting along, while having fun at the same time. We learned the very essence of building teams that accomplished a shared vision. Sadly, the adult children on your team today spend a great deal of time spinning their wheels trying to get ahead as opposed to building anything; except maybe dysfunction. Perhaps if more effort was put into honoring what we know works and less energy into setting up snares and or hoarding all the tools, we might have a more cohesive team.

The Case for Managers in the Sandbox

Did you know that managers today spend nearly one third of their time 'managing to' the underperformer on the team? That is about 12 hours a week spent on one person's inability or unwillingness to follow the rules of the sandbox. We will dive deeper into this issue later on in the book, but for now, consider this sandbox illustration: Imagine trying to build a castle without a bucket, the right shovel or water to hold it all together. If you as the manager spend one third of your time each day working to oversee *one* member of your team, how might that be pulling you off the goal? What tool (that would support the whole team to achieve the goal together) is missing?

When I go in to an organization and begin the conversation with a leader, we always begin the same way—with a question.

What is the number one challenge you face?

The answers I receive are similar, no matter the type of work or industry. And yet, I am continually impressed at how *creatively* the under-performance issues are avoided. In all transparency, I don't know that it's avoidant behavior or simply another reality blind spot. It is as if we can't look at the black hole we keep circling around in the office because we are too engulfed with trying to keep all the parts moving. Worse yet, leaders aren't noticing the disparate amount of work across the team as your high-functioning members pick up the slack for the *one* who regularly drops the shovel. Somewhere along the line, our managers today have become so used to managing *to the lack*, they struggle to see how the team's creative flow can be increased. If we as leaders are not fully equipped to lead our whole team at the same rate of speed, then we cannot ever fully realize our potential.

It's time to take back your bucket, fill it with water and put out the fire burning up your calendar called underperformance!

The Sandbox and Your Team

Whether you lead a team or are a member of one, how you honor the rules is no different. But before you can honor them as a highly-functioning adult member of a business team, you must re-engage with them. Some of you may be resisting the idea that there are *rules* to follow, but the reality is, we all have rules. Every aspect of life has rules. Either you follow them or you don't. There are rewards and consequences on either side of the line.

It's pointless to avoid naming the term, in which we all operate, as *rules*: call it what it is, or otherwise it's another tactic to keep the wheels spinning. I have worked with people on both sides of the debate on acknowledging rules, and some say they feel boxed in or limited by any set structure. They fear losing their creativity by being too regimented. They simply don't respect the work they do enough to honor the parameters that are in place to help us increase our capacity, get along and accomplish our goals. Look closely – those with that belief may be the ones perpetuating the underperformance issue in your office. If this is you, I invite you to look at how you benefit by avoiding the very set of tools that are in place to see you succeed at work.

Is there a person on your team who doesn't play well with others? If so, you have a pretty serious issue on your hands. Not only are they attacking your time and zapping your energy, but they are likely building a case for the whole team to feel demoralized and under-valued. Address the issue quickly. Have that bold conversation, otherwise the waiting game can have a very negative outcome.

You've heard the saying "if it's meant to be, it's up to me," right? Well, this applies to you no matter the position on the team. When it comes to affecting change, all your people are watching how you handle those who are not performing. They notice how you negotiate with the individual not adhering to the break time rules, or the habitually late or the leave-early employee. The resistant person who doesn't work well in the team needs to be addressed. And if it's going to happen, there is no time like the present.

Be cautious about how you publicly handle the renegade on the team, because your actions will likely speak volumes to the other members. The team has already had to find ways to work with (or around) the problem child, so don't add yourself to the list of people to navigate around. If you are distracted or spend an inordinate amount of time on the problem, you may miss the brilliance developing before your eyes. The highly functioning members of the team will keep things moving forward for you, yet only for a while if they are continually put on the back burner. Just because they do their jobs well, doesn't mean they don't need or want your input. They will look for ways to get your attention.

Please don't confuse 'getting attention' with high neediness. For those who honor the rules and structures set before them, they want to know they are making a difference; that they are valued on the team. Too often, leaders focus their attention so much on the one issue (or problem), that other members of the team suffer neglect and have little support. Remember, we don't want to lose our highly effective team members because of poor management of the underperformer.

While working with the president of a business unit for a leading technology company, we were discussing the challenges he had with one of his senior vice presidents. He was elaborating on the lack of trust that he had with this person's ability to do his job without being micro-managed. The behaviors that were being exhibited could have been misconstrued as passive or lack of accountability, but as we moved deeper into the discovery phase, we realized that the leadership capacity of this worker to lead his own team was significantly lower than what this position required.

This client was faced with two options: remove him from his position or marginalize his impact. Both options would require a restructuring of the team. You may be wondering why we didn't choose to coach this individual in an effort to increase their capacity. In many cases, that would be a viable solution.

However, in this situation it wasn't solely an issue of capacity. It was an issue of a willing heart—on both sides. The president had spent so much time checking on work assignments and readdressing unmet expectations that he was taking away valuable resources from the other members of the team. The underperforming worker was saying all the right things, but his words weren't lining up with his actions or output. He was, in a sense, sabotaging his own success and pulling the president's attention off the business unit as whole.

The effects on the other leaders were felt across the boardroom table. But the results most dramatically impacted the work of the down-line staff. One underperformer is much like the ripple effect a pebble has when tossed into the water. The direct impact hits only one spot, but the output is reverberating throughout the organization.

Consequently, other senior members of his team were forced to address the ripple effect caused by the poorly-performing senior vice president. As a leader, you are responsible for the entire team. You already know that, but it's important you see how much the distraction impacts everyone, evoking a reaction from the entire team.

As a leader, do you manage to the *one* or lead to address their ripple effect?

In the sandbox, if one kid wasn't playing nicely or they were stealing others' shovels making it hard to build the castle, the team took care of solving the problem together. But, in the workplace, the team doesn't necessarily have the authority or bandwidth to tackle the problem themselves. Often our teams just focus on ensuring that the ripple effect from the *one* has little impact on *their* unit, and they protect *their* employees.

For this business unit president, he learned something from Honorary Rule #5 when it came to his senior vice president. Yes, even adults litter the office environment and make it less than pleasurable to work in. Every member of your team is responsible to ensure we create a space that we can all succeed within. However, not everyone has the delegated authority from you, the leader, to impact change. The way you release and empower them all is important here. Or, maybe it is releasing the *one* litterbug, permanently.

In the next chapter, we'll break down the rules of the sandbox. It is a creative way of taking a fresh look at something you learned and used as a child, and yet somewhere along your journey, you let it go. Whether you are entrenched in battles with team members, silent saboteurs or egocentric leaders, getting back to the basics can be a great strategy for changing the culture and increasing the creative flow for everyone. Why not make a positive change to the environment where you spend the majority of your day?

Questions to Ask Yourself

Where are my underperformance blind spots?

Where have chaos and frustration sacrificed my creativity and flow?

When have I avoided boldly taking on an issue in an effort to keep the peace?

On a scale of 1 (low) - 10 (high) to what degree am I managing to the lack?

What do I believe to be true about my current situation?

Who is a resource for me to help make a change?

Questions to Ask Your Team (Individually and/or Confidentially)

What is the number one challenge you face?

As a leader on the team, what do you see as an underperformance issue?

Where do you spend most of your time?

On a scale of 1 (low) - 10 (high) what is the level of commitment from the entire team?

If you could change one thing about working within this team, what would it be?

3

DEFINING THE RULES OF THE SANDBOX

*"If your goal is to achieve any kind of altitude –
and it is – you'll have to do some serious digging."*
- Tammy Redmon

The rules are quite simple and easy to understand, in theory. We learned them as young children and figured out how to navigate them. Yet somewhere along the road to adulthood and cubicle nation, we left the very standards for engagement behind in an attempt to get ahead. Today, our teams are entrenched in a *just get by* or *do more with a whole lot less* ways of co-existing. Perhaps if we went back to an easier time of decision-making and negotiating, we'd see an increase in overall performance. Learning to navigate our offices today with multi-generational talent all around us can be difficult. But today, I take a stand for the simple rules we learned in pre-school to help us move forward as powerful negotiators and collaborators.

When you read through the rules of the sandbox, do so with both the left and right sides of your brain; engaging the creative force within *and* the analytic driver behind the scenes. View the rules as a shared set of blueprints we all use to build fantastic storylines. They serve as the foundation for our collective success.

Let's remember, we can of course, dig, shape, smooth, and even carry water with nothing but our own two hands. But having the right equipment and team with a shared vision will make our sand-castling experience infinitely more pleasurable. Here are the essentials:

Rule #1 - Don't Throw Sand

Whether you remember playing in the sandbox yourself as a kid, or now watch your own children navigating the neighborhood box, there's always *that* kid...the sand thrower. An eye full of sand was as reliable as the Sunday Times, and often, fodder for just as much drama. We'll call him Johnny; Johnny had his own agenda for how the play date was going to go. When he approached the sandbox, you could hear the collective deep breath from the other kids. And even the occasional protest to a parent. "Awe Mom...Do we have to?" Even though you knew the answer, you just had to ask; hoping this time Johnny would *not* be granted permission to play.

Why was he so unwanted?

Because Johnny had a bad habit: making you his sand target when he didn't get his way. He would lob a fistful of the fine grit morsels in the direction of whoever was either building a *better* castle, digging a *deeper* hole, designing a *more* creative mote, and the like. Bottom line – Johnny didn't like other kids doing anything before or better than him.

Back in the day as kids, we could get away with things that today's children (and adults) aren't afforded. We ganged up on Johnny and shut him down pretty quickly with some peer *influence*. Parents were a bit more hands-off at the sandbox when I grew up in the 70's. So we became very resourceful with the tools we had. It wasn't uncommon for our tribe to directly teach kids like Johnny *how* we played together (and how we didn't). We developed a system for moving the sand-thrower out of the box in a hot minute before his damage was too far spread. Some of the best tactics back then still work today in the adult world of teamwork, too.

In today's workplace, you have the proverbial sand thrower. The person who seems starved for attention or control – just like their 5-year-old alter ego – and stops at nothing to get the reaction they are aiming for: people complying and even cowering in fear.

On every team, whether at work, church or on a community board, you have a J.S.T. (Johnny Sand Thrower). The pay grade makes no difference, nor does the position of influence. A J.S.T. is not a respecter of position, pay grade or title. With ease and at will they lob insults or destructive comments. Your J.S.T. today often emits a passive-aggressive behavior pattern on the team; one who defies the deadlines and pushes the buttons of the other members of the team just to show their power. They promote their position and forward their agenda. It is no different than their 5-year-old counterpart. If, for some reason, the J.S.T. feels they are being out-performed by others on the team, no matter the output of work or results, they will lob the sand-bomb in the direction of the weakest link. The one who lobs sand doesn't necessarily go after the one who is excelling or building the better castle. No, they try to take out the other members of the team first because they are the bigger threats. Why are they the bigger threat? Because they support the vision and are doing the work of the team, and are likely making it difficult for Johnny the Sand Thrower to get what he wants most: *attention*.

Your J.S.T. definitely wants attention. They will stop at nothing and respect no boundaries, and nothing is off limits when it comes to getting *exactly* what they want.

Rule #2 - Don't Take Another Person's Shovel

The kid in the sandbox who was a habitual kleptomaniac (of the 4-year-old variety), was often the one who was completely oblivious to everything that was happening around her. She didn't mean to take away your shovel as if to cause you pain or to antagonize you. No, Suzy Shovel Stealer simply had her own needs to meet and would stop at nothing to get it done. If you had the small rake and she wanted to put a design on the outside of her castle, Suzy didn't see that you were using it to build a trench. What you were doing was of no concern and not even in her peripheral vision. The only thing Suzy Shovel Stealer saw was the rake in your hand. And she pushed her way to get it into her own.

Working with an S.S.S. is difficult, because children don't have the ability to control their selfish impulses. Much like Suzy, who reacts to her immediate need without contemplating the impact on others, the child on the receiving end often retaliates with fits and blows. Every mother in the neighborhood knows when the block S.S.S. has struck again. Someone ends up crying.

On our teams today, when Suzy Shovel Stealer makes her move, the effects are often reverberating throughout the office. Because much like the little 4-year-old's impulsivity, it comes out in adults on a much grander scale.

Some years ago, I had a unit director who was the S.S.S in the office. She was not fun to play with in cubicle nation. Her impulsive, *I want what I want and I want it now*, attitude was deafening to everyone around her. Remember the movie *Charlie and the Chocolate Factory* and that little darling, Veruca? "I want an oompa-loompa now!"

Our Suzy Shovel Stealer was much like that in personality. She was insistent on getting what she wanted, when she wanted it, no matter the cost to anyone else.

Her needs were set up on a high pedestal, and when she threw around her title with PhD behind her name, the overt temper-tantrum could be felt throughout the building.

I will never forget the day I took back the copier. The end of a deadline was approaching and I had to get a report off to the Governor's office by 5:00. The entire office was notified that I would have a high priority job printing on the color copier between set hours of the day, making it unavailable. Advance notice was given to all parties, including our S.S.S., whose assistant indicated there was no need for using this particular machine at the set time. Everyone knows who the person is in the office to take extra special care to work *around*; it's often the one who enjoys sabotaging for the sake of getting a great reaction.

About 2/3 of the way through my high-priority job, the door bursts open and in walks Suzy with 5 papers in hand. She demanded use of the copier, and for me to stop what I was doing.

I calmly explained that I had reserved the machine and would be using it until the job was completed. This didn't sit well for our Suzy...no. She began to increase in volume with a threatening tone. Then, right before she dropped her status and title, as if to compare it to mine, I took back the power in the room. I very directly stated that while she may have a PhD behind her name, I serve at the pleasure of the Governor and this project was going directly to his office. If she'd like me to let our boss know the project was late because her special "color" report on special "paper" that was for her eyes only, stopped the printing, I'd be happy to.

In response, I received one of my all-time favorite comeback lines from a Suzy Shovel Stealer, *"How dare you!!"*...and who cares what comes after a statement starting with those three words. When you are pushing back on a Suzy Shovel Stealer in the office, they often feel *they* are the victim, the most hard-working of all on the team. Anyone who needs to push their agenda forward because of title is not a team player. They are antagonistic and love getting reactions from people that they can use as bait the next time.

The way you handle a Suzy Shovel Stealer in the office is to take back the power by standing up and telling them their behavior is not going to work anymore. Place the accountability for the project success or failure back onto them. Stand firm on the goal, and kindly ask them to step aside. Typically, your S.S.S. is also conflict avoidant. That's why they throw temper tantrums and bully versus asking nicely. It gets them to their personal goal quicker and without having to negotiate or settle for less than what they might want. From that day forward, I didn't have another episode with Dr. S.S.S. in my office.

Rule #3 - Don't Knock Over Someone's Castle

In the office today there are three kinds of people:

- those that propel you forward,
- those who try to hold you back, and
- those who simply don't care about you.

The people who just don't care are like the sandbox kids who walked through it knocking over other people's creations. We could make the assumption that they are like Johnny Sand Thrower and want attention, but that's not exactly how I see it playing out over and over again.

The kid who knocked over everyone's creations was not at all concerned about status like our Suzy, or jealous like our Johnny. No, this kid, let's call him Nick, simply didn't care anything about the sandbox; not the rules and not the people. He just didn't get all the hype. There were other mountains to conquer and monkey bars to slay. Nick was the one who walked with his head down, as if hunting for his next battle, and it didn't matter what was in his way. He was singularly focused.

Remember the kid on the playground who would try to emulate the Karate Kid's famous "crane kick" like Ralph Macchio? He was the one who would stand in the middle of the field during recess and talk to himself (as if Mr. Miyagi were standing with him) and practice again and again. That singular focus was what made him odd...and even a little spooky as a kid. It could have given him a bully-like reputation, even at 6 years old. But truth be told, he was just the center of his own universe. Everything around him was white noise.

In the office today, your Nick the Castle Kicker may seem a little odd and doesn't fit the mold with the rest of the team. He is often the one who sits in the back of the meeting room and says very little during group discussions. But, when it comes to getting his work done, he never misses a deadline on his projects. However, his interpersonal skills are severely lacking. Nick's emotional awareness is commonly scored as very low on all the plethora of surveys we throw around the office today. *But he doesn't care.* The reports, and most often the people, are of no use to him.

He moves through the office singularly focused and anything in his path will be pushed aside or knocked over. Remember, he's not the bully. Nick *just doesn't care* about status; he cares about getting his job done and done *well*. He has rehearsed for this moment (just like on the playground), and he will plow through to achieve his results.

The difficulty about working with a Nick the Castle Kicker is how do you engage them with the team? A team can't have a lone, silo worker who is non-compliant to the ground rules and guiding statements that move everyone forward, and expect to transcend the goal – even if that one person is meeting their goals and deadlines.

You may be asking, "Why bother Nick?" If everyone is meeting their individual goals, then we all win, yes? In theory, yes, but remember, the Nick in your office moves oblivious through his day, knocking into and over whatever may be in his path. He is unaware that others have goals to meet too. He may withhold information that is required for the team project to move forward because he doesn't believe in its value. Or worse, he may change the data or the outcome to fit his perception of what *should be* because he really didn't agree in the meeting when the target or outcome was discussed.

Remember, Nick the Castle Kicker moves through the sandbox on his own terms and mission, and is oblivious to the needs of others. It's not to be mean or purposely sabotage, he is just singularly focused. You as the leader get to help him see how his contribution matters to the whole organization. Nick can build the *widget*, and does so with a high degree of excellence, but he needs your help to understand how his part fits into the bigger picture. Help him expand his vision, and your whole team will rise up.

Rule #4 - Share Your Tools

Every kid in Kindergarten learned quickly to share their crayons. Teacher taught us that rule on day one. Even so, it was so darn hard! My brand new crayon box had *my* name printed neatly on the front, and I was never going to break a single one; something I couldn't trust with the other kids. I remember thinking if we all have our own box of crayons, why did we have to share? But Mrs. Alsop was pretty clear about her rules, and I knew if I didn't follow them I wouldn't get a chance to be the wake-up fairy at nap time. Being the wake-up fairy was the reward carrot dangled in front of me! We learn very early the power of negotiation to get our reward or consequence.

In the sandbox, some kids brought spoons and bowls from the kitchen. Other kids brought bright, colorful buckets and shovels made especially for the sand. We all came with tools of various shapes, sizes and uses. It only took a moment to identify the specific purpose for each tool, often sparking a great debate over which sand tool was best for the new feature on our latest creation. Inevitably, the kids who brought buckets were the ones who trumped decision making for the whole box. They had the best equipment for the job.

Maybe it was its bright yellow color, or maybe it was because theirs was the sturdiest one made especially for the sandbox, but either way, the best bucket won the debate every time. And every other kid in the box wanted to try their hand at stacking the perfect tower with the best bucket.

Unfortunately, not all kids, buckets or even crayons are created equal. To relinquish the prized item in the sandbox was often fodder for a few tears and hurt feelings. To a small child, thinking of sharing their prized possession is difficult, let alone do. As an adult on a team, it's not much different, though we learn later in life how to cope with sharing challenges.

When I work with teams who struggle with sharing resources, equipment and prized possessions, I expose their lack of trust and heightened fear. Teams today are not much different than the neighborhood kids in the sandbox of yesteryear. We need trust to feel safe. We need to feel safe to trust.

When my nephew visited our house as a small boy, my son would go through his room beforehand and put all his prized toys out of reach. It wasn't because he couldn't share; other kids from preschool came over frequently, and he never felt compelled to hide any of his toys. He didn't feel comfortable sharing special things with his cousin. My nephew knew that his cousin had some pretty special toys, and he was on a mission to find the stash.

One day, I listened outside the playroom door to their conversation. At just 3 years old, my son blurted out to his cousin, "No, you can't play with that, you don't take care of my toys!" Tears quickly followed, because they were both hurt; hurt by the accusation and hurt by the fear.

In our workplace today, when we don't share our resources with one another, we must ask ourselves why. What stops us from wanting to give our tools, our knowledge and our time to another person on the team? Why is it only that *one* individual that we won't share with? It is imperative to ask yourself these questions before an explosion of hurtful words break forth.

Your team may feel ownership over their own pieces of the toolbox. They may not trust that you or other members of the team will take care of it the same way they do. As the leader, the greatest gift to give your team is the ability to trust one another and the tools to communicate effectively when trust is disappointed. Without open dialogue, there is no trust; which elicits fear in every member. Fear is the counterpart to underperformance.

Honorary Rule #5 - Don't Eat the Sand

As I mentioned before, I ask the question about the number one rule of the sandbox at every speaking event. It is one of my favorite moments with the audience, because it opens up their child's mind and evokes fond memories. At one event, filled with members of a Senior Human Resource Management group, a lady blurted out from the middle of the room, "Don't eat the sand!" Of course, I was curious where that random response came from, so I inquired further only to receive a hysterical response.

*"Because the neighborhood cat uses it as
a litter box!"*

The visual was quite enough to evoke a great deal of laughter, littered with a number of disgusted facial expressions and moans.

Let me be brief with this honorary rule. If you have a team member who is littering your sandbox at work with things that stink and are less than pleasing, choose not to partake in their antics. Have a bold conversation about the less-than-harmonious (or even unhealthy) behavior and extinguish it quickly. These behaviors are a form of silent sabotage that can have devastating impact for your team.

Questions to Ask Yourself

What rule do I most embrace?

What rule do I resist?

Do I know the rules of our team sandbox?

If I were to make one change to better get along with the team, what would I change?

Is there a bold conversation I need to have? With whom, and when will I have it?

Questions to Ask About My Team

What attitudes do I see that cause fear amongst the team?

How is the team at sharing their resources and tools with one another?

Who needs help in seeing their part and contribution to the bigger picture?

Who on the team acts as a silent saboteur?

What bold conversation needs to happen to bring the rules of engagement into alignment with the team?

4

EMOTIONS AND THE WORKPLACE

"Your emotional awareness and ability to handle feelings will determine your success and happiness in all walks of life, including family relationships."
–John Gottman

Our emotions, not our thoughts, motivate us. Without an awareness of what we feel, it's impossible to fully understand our own behavior, appropriately manage our emotions and actions, and accurately *read* the wants and needs of others.

Whether we're aware of them or not, emotions are a constant presence in our lives, influencing everything we do.

Emotional awareness means knowing what you are feeling and *why*. It's the ability to identify and express what you are feeling from moment to moment and to understand the connection between your feelings and the actions they cause.

Beyond the personal benefits, emotional awareness also has another component, which reaches outward: the ability to understand what others are feeling and to empathize with them.

Emotional awareness involves the ability to:

- Recognize your moment-to-moment emotional experience
- Handle all of your emotions without becoming overwhelmed

Emotional awareness helps you:

- Recognize who you are: what you like, what you don't like and what you need
- Understand and empathize with others
- Communicate clearly and effectively
- Make wise decisions based on the things that are most important to you
- Get motivated and take action to meet goals
- Build strong, healthy and rewarding relationships

The ability to express and control our own emotions is important, but so is our ability to understand, interpret, and respond to the emotions of others. Imagine a world where you couldn't understand when a friend was feeling sad or when a co-worker was angry. Psychologists refer to this ability as emotional intelligence, and some experts even suggest it can be more important than a person's IQ.

When you're aware and in control of your emotions, you think clearly and creatively; manage stress and challenges; communicate well with others; and display trust, empathy and confidence. But when emotions get out of control, you'll spin into confusion, isolation and negativity. By recognizing and harnessing your emotions, you can gain control over the way you react to challenges, improve your communication skills and enjoy more fulfilling relationships. This is the life-changing power of developing emotional awareness.

One of the best stories I can share about the power of harnessing your emotions is when I worked with the president of a technical college and his team. I was brought in to do some work with the team around their accountability and the way they communicated with one another.

In my first meeting, the president was telling me about his team and what he believed to be some of the issues. He highlighted one specific VP on his team. This man was seeking promotion and was continually passed by. The president told me, "It's because John has no emotional intelligence. He failed the test we gave him." That broke my heart to hear! Not because he *failed* the test but because now he had been *labeled* as emotionally unaware from some silly assessment. As I inquired about John's behaviors and what might be limiting his performance, the president didn't have much to offer. He just kept describing John as cold, unattached to his peers and his direct reports, and people had no desire to be around him. At one point the president shared that John was 'too fragile' to approach.

You see, John wasn't having emotional outbursts, he was just showing no emotional evidence at all, to anyone. Not joy, sorrow, frustration or even anger. He was stoic, making him unapproachable.

There are various types of emotional unawareness, and sometimes we contain our emotions so much in relationships that we push others away in the process. We make ourselves so prickly because we tell people with our actions and body language that we don't care about them or don't want them around. Please don't mistake emotional awareness to only be associated with people who are boisterous or outwardly aggressive. That does cause breakdown, yes, but so does emotional vacancy. And when you are working in the sandbox with someone emotionally vacant, it attracts distrust very much the same way the boisterous bully does in the office.

So why is this thing called emotional awareness important for you to explore? This skill makes you a better team member and stronger leader, while at the same time increasing your overall self-efficacy. Strengthening the system that our emotions operate within plays a major role in how we perceive situations and how we behave in response to different situations.

Bottom line: the more aware you are of your responses to self and to others impacts the way you operate the dynamic human-being you contend with every single day – YOU.

According to psychologist Albert Bandura, self-efficacy is "the belief in one's capabilities to organize and execute the courses of action required to manage prospective situations." In other words, self-efficacy is a person's belief in his or her ability to succeed in a particular situation. Bandura described these beliefs as determinants of how people think, behave, and feel (1994).

Are you curious how the topic of emotional awareness and research on self-efficacy is important to our teams and the way we navigate the tides of cubicle nation? Here is why.

When our team members increase their ability to understand self, first, they expand their awareness to the people (and their reactions) around them. In the confines of your office, it increases harmony and ownership like nothing else I have ever seen. When we expose our work units to the body of work around self-efficacy, we see performance increase by leaps and bounds. Next to doing values work, there is no other tool I have used in organizations that propels the communication, cohesiveness and goal achievement growth of a team faster than self-efficacy work.

The role of self-efficacy in the workplace:

Virtually all of us can identify goals we want to accomplish, things we would like to change and achievements we're aiming for. However, most people also realize that putting these plans into action is not quite so simple. Bandura and others have found that an individual's self-efficacy plays a major role in how goals, tasks, and challenges are approached.

People with a strong sense of self-efficacy:

- View challenging problems as tasks to be mastered
- Develop deeper interest in the activities in which they participate
- Form a stronger sense of commitment to their interests and activities
- Recover quickly from setbacks and disappointments

People with a weak sense of self-efficacy:

- Avoid challenging tasks
- Believe that difficult tasks and situations are beyond their capabilities
- Focus on personal failings and negative outcomes
- Quickly lose confidence in personal abilities

Self-efficacy is often an overlooked, but critical component to successfully completing a task in the workplace. In order to develop a more effective workforce, managers benefit by having a comprehensive understanding of self-efficacy and what factors affect levels of self-efficacy in employees.

Two Levels of Efficacy

There are two levels of efficacy in the workplace:

1. Self-Efficacy

Self-efficacy is a person's belief about his/her chances of successfully accomplishing a specific task. It arises from the acquisition of complex cognitive, social, linguistic, and/or physical skills through experience.

2. Collective Efficacy

Collective efficacy is a group's perceptions of their ability to achieve results together (Bandura, 1982). It is the collective belief that the group shares and is therefore emanating from the group rather than the individual.

In the workplace, both self-efficacy and collective efficacy are important when engaging in individual, collaborative and group-based tasks. How an individual views their own capabilities affects not only their personal work, but the work they engage in with the team. Additionally, the team's collective view of their capability not only affects their work as a team but also what each individual on the team feels capable of executing.

Let's break this down a little further. When members of your team can see themselves as goal-achieving, successful collaborators who can work with autonomy, they will do just about anything for you. However, *before* they can create for you, they need a new picture of who they are and what their end result success looks like.

When your team can see their own task's success before it starts, their ability to exceed expectations becomes your reality. Focusing on the project's completion and measuring their actions toward the end goal becomes easier, and so does supporting those around them to do the same. If the picture of the outcome isn't clear, wheels spin aimlessly and often delay the process. Get a clear picture by asking this question with the end in mind:

"What will it look like when you complete this project?"

Then wait for the answer to emerge. Keep asking them, "What else?" until they have nothing else to add. Inside the clarity and awareness around *their* contribution lies the outcome *you* want. The picture of success has been built.

Did you know our words create pictures in our minds? Or that we move in the direction of the dominant picture? For many people walking in and out of their cubicle on a daily basis, they are self-sabotaging their ability to be a success by the words they speak, murmur and mumble. With each word spoken, a mind picture is created which evokes some kind of emotion. Try it. Say a word and pay attention to what picture pops up in your mind.

When I say, "Pink Elephant," what pops into your mind? If I mention Maui, Hawaii, what image does that evoke? What emotion charges up on the inside? During the next conversation you have when someone else is talking, notice what picture comes to mind.

You see, when we have a low sense of self, our tide table for emotional awareness is at a minus 3 most days. We automatically perpetuate what we don't want until we change our viewpoint. How? By getting a new picture of where we are going. By speaking and drawing attention to what you **don't want**, what you don't want becomes the focus. This will cause momentum to move in the wrong direction, because you are actually doing the opposite of what you think you are doing. And so every member of your team becomes stuck on the round-a-bout of *lack, less than* and *not good enough.*

Do you see that if the members of your unit are locked onto what won't work, things will never change? How the plethora of rationale for failure has created a self-fulfilling prophecy? This is one important factor when it comes to collective efficacy for your team's success. This might just be your magic bullet that truly gets your team off the spinning round-a-bout and into the high performance lane. Do the important work regarding how your team sees themselves, sees the work they do and how they see the others they do the work with: it expands our expectations for increase and new possibilities.

Avoiding looking at individual and collective view points of the work, tasks and projects you have only perpetuates the problems you have been contending with. Underperformance issues will move deeper into the org chart while your hair moves off your head, being pulled out from stress; either way... it's not good!

Let's recap. We have just spent time looking at how being emotionally aware improves our relationship with self and with others. We broke down the research around self-efficacy, both individually and collectively. And we connected the dots between our words and the pictures they create that move us toward or away from our goal. So how do you apply all of this rich information to your team? It starts with how you apply it to *yourself*.

Note to reader: Your team can sniff out the vanity of a selfish motive or double standard like a hunting dog on the trail of their next prey. It is imperative that you do your own work first.

Be willing to listen to the view from other people's chairs.

In many instances I have seen teams begin to open up their awareness to self by the way their leader models the transparency of their own change. Leaders, your team is watching every move you make; some watch for reasons of curiosity and others simply to confirm their case that you aren't who you say you are or aren't out for the best interest of the whole. Now, let me just say, not every member of your team is looking and waiting for you to fail. Consider that some people want to see you succeed due to your sustained effort. Why? Because it raises their belief that they, too, possess the capabilities to master comparable activities to succeed.

Often, the leaders I work with believe expressing their emotions is something that is not appropriate at work. We tend to tie emotions to personal life and try to keep the line between work and personal very clear.

A few years ago, I worked with an executive director of an agency who, while highly respected by those he supervised, was a mystery to his peers. They saw him as distant, uncaring of the mission and goals of the organization and lacking a team approach to the work. He was a *lone wolf*, they would say. When it came to doing an in-depth, 360° review on the leadership team, his report was the trigger for the coaching. Why? It wasn't that he didn't do his work and do it well, but his lack of emotional connection with the others spurred people to not trust him.

Remember, it is not the sheer intensity of emotional and physical reactions that is important but rather how they are perceived and interpreted.

This executive was unaware how strongly his aloof, distant approach to *team* pushed people away from everything he brought to the table. Together we worked on looking at the ways he communicated non-verbally, and how they either drew others in or pushed them away. We created an environment where some safe conversations could happen so that he could hear from others how they perceived his actions. This guy had *no idea* that keeping so calm, cool and always collected, even in difficult conversations, was continually rejecting others around him. The people you work with really do want to see just a little bit of healthy emotion from you. If you are always holding things in, you don't seem human to them. It can come across as judgmental and cold.

The emotions of others that we perceive can carry a wide variety of meanings. And as people perceive you, they make judgments: either you are safe or to be avoided. You might think that the overtly angry person in the office is the one that is avoided most intensely, right? Not true. Those people are easier to *read* (body language) so we can mentally put them in a box and know how to approach them. But the people who withhold emoting – the good, bad or ugly – in the office are greatly feared because we don't know how to approach or respond to them. It makes it very difficult to partner with someone who lacks an emotional connection.

Sadly, this executive made a decision to collect his marbles and move on to a different playing field. He resigned and moved to a new agency where no one knew him and he could start fresh. The reality is that he could not address his own emotional awareness challenges in an effort to increase a positive view from the others' chair. He left a job he loved and a career that he worked over 20 years to build in order to protect himself from making a change in how he played in the sandbox.

Questions to Ask Yourself

What are my strengths and my limitations?

How do I handle stressful situations?

What do I do when someone comes in with a problem?

How do I develop rapport with people?

How would my colleagues describe me?

On a scale of 1 (low) to 10 (high) how do I rate myself in the following:

Self-Awareness: the ability to recognize your own emotions.

Self-Management: the ability to balance your needs and the needs of others.

Social Awareness: the ability to tune into other people's emotions and concerns.

Relationship Management: the ability to get along well with others, manage conflict, inspire and influence people.

Questions to Ask Your Team

What are our strengths and our limitations?

What do we do when someone comes in with a problem?

What is it that the people on our team still need and how do we think they feel?

Colleagues, how would you describe me?

5

COMMUNICATION IS 50/50

*"The single biggest problem in communication
is the illusion that it has taken place."*
– George Bernard Shaw

My absolute favorite topic, and the one thing that lights me up on the inside most when working with clients, is *communication*. I believe it is the single, most impacting tool teams can wield, but it is also the most under-utilized tool of them all. Every relationship breakdown begins, at some level, because of a lack of or a break in communication. When I work with leaders, I spend the greatest amount of time with them on communication; even the ones that think they are already exceptional communicators.

Communication is probably the one topic that leaders think of as *low priority* on the scale of things needing help in their organization. Ask the rest of the people in the company what the greatest need is for improvement, however, and hands down their resounding answer is communication. It seems we know, but don't do. We're accustomed to *knowing* communication is important, but rarely *make* actual improvements in this area.

Commonly, it takes a big challenge, problem or issue to arise before we finally take a look at how we are going to communicate it or address it. Sadly, this approach for some is too little, too late. My hope is that this chapter will show you how to more effectively communicate with the people on your team, even when you don't want to. It's time to gain skills and insights to address the big hairy issues (that I call *"the Pink Elephant"*) in the office before there are casualties from avoiding it.

Recently, a Fortune 500 company brought me in to work with their executive team during their annual, off-site meeting. In the initial interview with the CEO, I learned that there was a decision made that had the potential to take the company to even greater heights in the future. It would require the executives' support to gain the momentum to make the change. The concern was how the other members of the leadership team would receive the change the CEO wanted to implement.

For some companies, their CEOs make sweeping changes without aligning their team and have a *'just deal with it'* approach. Honestly, sometimes that is necessary. However, and quite thankfully in this case, this leader saw the value in getting his team into agreement and harmony around this big change *before* it happened so they could address any resistance up front, avoiding sabotage down the road.

While at this off-site meeting, we did in fact run into some high emotions around what was coming for this company. However, we had done work in advance to secure the key points of what we were communicating, what the expectations were and what powerful requests needed to be made to the team. Part of the initial challenge was getting the CEO to be crystal clear in the *how* and *what* of the communication, and if we were met with emotional push back, how to use my role and purpose on the team for facilitating that communication process. Often, I stand in the threshold for the difficult conversations to happen as a neutral third party there to help both sides see and hear clearly from the other.

Communication is 50/50

For years I have studied the way people communicate. I have looked at how culture, gender, role and past experiences affect the style and manner in which we send and receive communication. And over my career, I have determined that all communication is 50/50—but not how you might be thinking it is. My 50/50 rule means equal parts being equally responsible for both sides of the communication: both sending and receiving. Let me break it down.

When in a conversation with an individual, the way I deliver a message and the ability for that message to be received (successfully) is equally my responsibility—no matter the side of the table I sit on. If, at any point, both parties do not see their equal ownership in the success of the communication, we have both failed. When I deliver a message to someone, it is imperative that I first take account for the *what* and *why* of it. What do I need to say? Why do I need to say it?

If, at any point, I am emotionally charged, because "*Gosh darn it, this bloke needs to hear what I am going to say...,*" then I have just abandoned half my responsibility. Emotions will come up in our conversations, yes, but if I am unaware of my reactions to them or the *why* behind my reaction, then I close myself off from receiving from the other party. However, if I can identify that my emotional temperature is rising because my values are being pressed upon and I can state that to the other person in a respectful manner (or simply ask to table the conversation until a later time when I have cooled down), then our chances for a successful communication just increased.

The 50/50 rule of engagement is simply put: you are 50% responsible for how you send the message and 50% responsible for how it is received. The other party you are in the dialogue with shares in the other half of each side with you.

This is, for sure, a new way of looking at

communication with members of our team. Some of the best work I have seen teams do is in the area of shared responsibility with every encounter. Why? Because we are raised to only think about and consider *our* side of the communication. Now when we look at it as an equally-shared responsibility, it is a paradigm shift. If a message is delivered and dropped like a hot potato, and then you walk away, you failed. It is your responsibility to ensure that it was received *and* understood. On the other side, it is the other person's responsibility to own their reaction to it. That is *key*. We own how we both react to what is being said.

When we deliver a message, there are often hidden signals that we give off in our body language and facial expressions. We may be unaware of how our body language and expressions may push people away or cause them to reject what we are saying, altogether. This one simple adjustment in communication could make a huge difference. As someone who is notorious for their facial expressions, this has been one of my greatest areas for growth and one of my greatest sensitivities.

We will talk further about body language later on in the chapter, but for now let's talk about how communication is hijacked by an ill-placed frown line. Knowing this about myself, I make sure to ask the other person how they received my information or message. If I notice any withholding from them or notice them physically pushing away, I am compelled to engage them further for understanding. Too often, people will say, "Yep, got it," when they really aren't committed to or willing to take on the information that was just delivered. They are just trying to get away from you. In that case, the other person has failed their part of the 50/50 rule. You see, we each have ownership in the success and fail points of every encounter.

Several years ago, I was sitting at a boardroom table with a CEO of one of the top 25 Seattle-based companies and his executive board. We were discussing doing some performance and communication work with the entire company. In advance of the meeting, we had conducted some interviews with his team to understand the view from their chairs; what they thought were strengths and weaknesses from the top down.

When I walked into that meeting, I stood to the side and watched the folks as they came in and where they selected to sit. You can learn a lot about a group by watching their seat selection. When the CEO walked in, eyes went down and talking stopped. He did his best to try to engage them in dialogue, but nearly everyone held back their comments.

As we dove into the objective for the meeting, the CEO's only concern was hearing the findings of the staff interviews. As we began to deliver the findings, it wasn't long before I understood why his team was avoiding eye contact with him and everyone else at the table. Mr. CEO was not there for the good of the whole. He was there to look good *to* the whole and to the consultants sitting at the table. He was unwilling to listen to any feedback that suggested his people, in general, weren't happy at work.

As I did my very best to open up dialogue, he was having nothing to do with it. He just wanted to know the '*who said what*' in the feedback process, and then his language got very colorful. Try as I might with him, he was not open to hearing *anything* he didn't want to hear, which confirmed all the feedback we received in our interviews. This also confirmed why people didn't engage him in the room and kept their heads down. This CEO only wanted to hear what confirmed his picture of the company he founded—nothing else.

At one point he blurted out to me that if *the people* would just do what he does and follow his model, performance wouldn't be an issue. Little did he realize that they actually *were* following his model and performance was dropping, quickly. Then he started picking at people around the table. This meeting went from uncomfortable to a pressure cooker, rapidly.

You see, he only cared about what he was saying and was not open to hearing what others were saying or how they were receiving the information. In cases where you have a rather bullheaded individual, who happens to drop (often) that he built the company, signs the paychecks and rules his team by fear, they are not going to easily change. The purpose of the meeting wasn't to change him right there and then, but if we didn't turn it around quickly, the chance to change the working environment would never come.

I wish I could tell you the outcome of that meeting was successful, but I am sure you can see why it was not. He did not want to cooperate and play well with others, or be open to hear the viewpoint of those willing to give their feedback. He thought I was rather pushy, and that if his people (those at the table) had a problem with him, they would tell him directly, right then. For an uncomfortable amount of time, he asked folks at the table to chime in, and of course they elected not to. You cannot have shared communication with someone who is unwilling to receive. Not surprisingly, that CEO had a high rate of turnover in his executive team the year following our meeting and the trickle-down effect was very damaging.

If you work for someone like this, I wish you well. I would offer this advice: do your best to know your 'why' behind the reason you do the work you do. Be persistent in sharing that why with your CEO. More often than not these types of leaders just want to know that the people on their team have their back and will protect them to some degree. Know that the road to success for you will be rather stressful, so you must have a solid self-care plan in place to keep up with the demands.

Perhaps that story resonates because you might

be one of those leaders that don't want to listen. You just want people to sit down, keep quiet and do their jobs.

You may be building a solid foundation for a demoralized team with that approach, but that will only work for a while. The CEO's company in the story had great success and had been around Seattle for decades. But when he reached his *ceiling of complexity* as a leader, he ruled from a place of fear; pushing his people out rather than empowering his people forward. If your people fear you, go back to the rule of 50/50 and be open to having dialogue where you just listen. Seek to understand first, and then create your plan for change.

Remember, 50/50 communication means I am equally responsible for sending and receiving information. If either side is not clear, it is up to me to get it straightened out. If everyone on your team operated from this place of equality, our performance numbers would skyrocket, as wheel-spin lessens and clarity reigns.

One last thought on 50/50 communication. We've spent our entire lives communicating. As babies, we are communicating from the moment we are born, and our parents learned quickly how to respond depending on what we were delivering. As children, we learn how to get what we want from people with our actions and words. As young people moving into adulthood though, something changes. The antics or tactics that worked as children no longer work effectively in our adult relationships, which can be a difficult hurdle to overcome. It is up to us to make that course correction.

In a work environment, we often see people exhibit repelling, childlike behaviors. We box those people in quickly and want to avoid them at all costs. But as a partner on the team, and as someone who now shares in the success of every interaction, you can truly benefit from helping others to understand how you want to be communicated with.

My main point when it comes to communication is this: if you approach every communication with a WIIFM (*what's in it for me*) perspective, you will more often than not end up on the short end of the stick. As a leader, your people will not trust you, and you will likely have high turnover, costing you time and money. As a team member, you will feel like the weight of every project is on your shoulders, causing frustration and leaving you feeling broke, busted and disgusted at work.

We spend more time at work with our coworkers than we do our own families. Why wouldn't we want to take every step necessary to be bold, heart-centered and open in every encounter? Make the decision today to share both sides of the next conversation, even the uncomfortable one. Who are you not to?

Questions to Ask Yourself

When have you failed at communicating?

When have you felt that you weren't heard when trying to communicate?

What was your response?

How do you view your responsibility with communication?

When you need to be that voice of truth for someone else, how do you approach it?

What do others around you say about your style of communication?

What do you see happening when applying the 50/50 rule on your team?

How can you prepare your team for this style of ownership?

6

HELP ME UNDERSTAND

"Shallow understanding from people of good will is more frustrating than absolute misunderstanding from people of ill will." – Martin Luther King, Jr.

People ask me every day how to tackle a difficult conversation in the workplace. They often think because I coach on communication and talk about it so much that I must be comfortable with having tough conversations. The truth is, I am probably just as uncomfortable as the next person. I just don't shy away from it because I know its value. As I have *learned* how to approach the most irksome situations with finesse, it first required a deep look into myself. The success between every encounter starts and ends with me.

For some of you, that thought may be difficult to wrap your mind around. But I believe it to be true. We are only responsible for ourselves, our reactions, our temperament, our responses, and our feelings. No one can make you feel poorly unless you allow them to. But somehow in the world of cubicle nation, we have a lot of people wandering around feeling powerless and ineffective, hiding out in the break room to avoid others at all costs. They feel like the victim working in a *'have to or else'* world. At the core of the passive behavior, with the *'just get by'* time clock in their head, is a wounded person who just needs to have a truthful conversation with someone to take back their personal power. Years later, that person could still be having the same problems, because they avoid the conversation.

If you want a change:
• Stop avoiding the solution
• Have that conversation
• Tackle that issue

While I was working on my own communication style, reforming my passive-aggressive tendencies while in the confines of a cubicle world, I learned the power of three little words. I will share them in a moment. Getting ahold of those words, and using them daily, transformed the way I viewed my relationships and the way I accomplished my work within a team. It began with how I viewed *me* and how I viewed the people I worked with. It also took a great deal of work to see my value and the value of the people around me.

I was driven from an early age by the WIIFM (what's in it for me) theory. Everything I put out there was to produce a return for me, myself and I.

Through the years, that attitude served me well, and made me appear as an over-achiever. My bosses loved me; my co-workers avoided me. Why? Because I was relentless to get the job done ahead of schedule and to exceed all expectations. However, my co-workers avoided me, and I was the fodder for many water-cooler conversations. What changed for me? A few things did. Going through college and studying inter-cultural communications opened my eyes to the fact that even if we all look like we are from the same culture, we in fact are not.

Every family creates their own culture, and as a young adult, I was communicating the way I was conditioned in my home life. But at work, my relationships were strained. My co-workers didn't understand my style and I didn't care to understand theirs. Styles were a barrier to getting what I wanted and needed.

I also discovered that I was very emotionally unaware. I did not have a clear understanding of my impact on others. I knew that if I was getting my job done I was a good girl, but I couldn't understand why I wasn't being invited out to lunch with others from the office. That hurt.

My change began when I became aware of my impact on others; on my co-workers and even on my personal relationships. After years of feeling powerless, I wasn't having the outcomes I most desired. I looked into what was in my way, and as most people discover, it was none other than *me*, my attitude and my response to others. Perhaps this is why I love working with people on their own communication challenges; especially those that mask it as somebody else's problem in the office. Those are the most valiant efforts to preserve self-satisfaction while achieving the self-fulfilling prophecy of 'not good enough' and 'nobody likes me' position. The bottom-line is I truly understand it all at a very personal level; I have done my own work and now walk the talk, helping others escape the binding chains of self-preservation.

Years ago, I learned the power of three little words that changed the way I entered every single conversation; the good and the bad. They changed the way I showed up at work, played in the sandbox with my teams and even the way I parented my children.

Today, you too get to learn those words and how to use them so that you can start slaying the dragons in your office called conflict-avoidant, passive-aggressive, underperformance and just-get-by. More importantly, you get to take back your personal power!

What comes next has so much power in it that I caution you on how you use this next tool. Before you just start wielding this sandbox sword around the office, I want you to pause and visit the Emotional Awareness quiz at the end of this book first. This change tool requires you to be very aware of how you approach yourself and then how you approach others. These three words transformed the way I communicate. Now they can do the same for you.

Help Me Understand...

Yes, that is it. Simple, direct and to the point. Those three powerful words are a game-changer in the workplace. I see it every single day with my clients.

You might be wondering how to use them. Well, they are tied very closely to the last chapter on the 50/50 rule of communication. Now that we understand our shared responsibility in every conversation, we can use these words to aid us in getting to resolution when conflict shows up. "Help me understand." It's one thing to know you share in the ownership of the successful outcome, but what about the times when your teammate does not? Insert the *help me understand* power tool and watch what happens.

Note to reader: knowing your emotional pressure points is key here when you first begin using this communication tool. People who are not used to the new, improved communicator that you are becoming will still respond and react to you in their old behavior patterns. It takes time for others to adjust their picture of who you are in the workplace, so be gentle to self and others here.

When my clients have communication break-downs with co-workers, we coach around our expectations. We walk out what the intended outcome is or needs to be and then equip them with their next best question. It always starts with *help me understand* as the lead in. One client of mine named Joe, found this tool to be the most helpful, and also the most frustrating.

I remember the call from him like it was yesterday. He shared about using this powerful question in a meeting, but he felt like it was doubling and tripling the time it took to get resolution. Even his team was commenting on wishing he would just get to the point and tell them what he wanted. However for this president, just telling his team hadn't worked since he had taken over the position some 9 months prior to the catastrophic breakdown. Joe found his team lacking in accountability at every turn.

When he tried to get them aligned with what accountability meant, they felt that he was pressuring them to do it his way. When he asked the team to identify for him what accountability meant to them, they took three weeks to give him a multiple page document on their collective definition of accountability. Joe was exasperated!

He had a team that would put goals and targets forward for their units only to never come close to hitting them. They felt bullied when he tried to ask them what got in their way. More importantly, he wondered why they didn't tell him before the deadlines that they weren't going to hit the target. Joe was speechless. He was at a complete loss as a newly appointed leader in the organization on how to lead people who thought it was totally fine to *not* achieve the intended goal, and blame others for the outcome.

Joe tried a new approach. He lessened his direct communication with them to a more inclusive approach that included seeking to understand. Not to understand why they failed or didn't honor their commitments, but to understand the thinking behind it all. And yes, it slowed the cadence of the meetings so that all minds could align to the change that he needed to see.

As someone who was very business and strategy focused, leading a team who was deeply entrenched in self-preservation and avoidant behavior, he needed to find a new strategy to get to the root of the problem. So we released the *help me understand* at the beginning of every conversation he needed to have when expectations weren't met. And for Joe, this happened a lot!

While in the beginning it took longer to get through meetings and often left people feeling annoyed, in the end it *transformed* the way everyone communicated. More importantly, it changed the way people came into meetings to deliver results. You see, when Joe shifted his approach and became consistent with the new way he ran meetings, his team knew how to come prepared.

While it took longer to implement at the beginning, they now move swiftly through meetings, and each are using the *help me understand* questioning process. They have increased their performance by leaps and bounds and have finally settled on what accountability means to them.

How do you use it?

Using this three-word power tool is quite simple. When you are in a conversation or need to have one, identify what you want or need to know as an outcome. Then start your questioning process with *help me understand,* fill in the last part of the question with your need or outcome. Here is what some questions might sound like:

Sam, help me understand what you had hoped the outcome would be?

Delores, help me understand – we agreed on achieving a 27 % increase this quarter, and that our progress would be reported monthly.

Rachel, help me understand how pushing the project out before we had agreement on the targets would help the team be successful?

Now, there are more variations to this questioning process than I can detail here in this chapter. And you may be concerned that the tone might sound sarcastic or even belittling as I had one client tell me. It won't if your intention for a successful outcome is clear versus making the other person wrong. When we enter into a conversation to seek understanding, first we must set aside our assumptions about *who's right vs. who's wrong*. If not, it certainly will sound condescending to your team.

My invitation to you is this. Start this transformation with a conversation about the change. Tell your team upfront that you are going to ask questions to gain understanding so that you know how to best lead them. If you are doing this from the motive of helping everyone succeed, you will gain traction quickly as opposed to putting people down.

How to Communicate the Good, Bad and Ugly

There are times as leaders when we need to be bold truth tellers. We must speak to uncomfortable situations, and hopefully we get to celebrate many victories also. How we communicate in these times can be trying, but it's when the most transparency is required. Your team will receive really tough information from you when you are being transparent in the information you share.

Now, allow me be clear. There are things that we are *not* to share with our people. I am not advocating that we open up the books on the business for all to see and share the nitty-gritty details of day to day happenings. However, I am advocating that if you can't share it, say you can't. Your people know if a cutback or layoff is coming before you have even agreed to the terms or selected the people. They know. Your team knows if a new set of operational procedures is coming down and they just want to hear it from you as their leader first. Communicating the good, bad and ugly is necessary, and it's all in the *how* you do it that counts for your people. When you have tough news to share, you need to know that the way you deliver it will either keep people performing or lock them up in fear.

More often than not, teams that are the most severely demoralized are those who have been working under leaders who lack transparency and truth-telling ability.

Some of the greatest leaders I have studied and worked with have an impeccable ability to deliver tough information and have everyone feeling honored in the process. They operate from a sense of doing what is right, but also head directly into the path of the storm before it makes landfall. They choose not to avoid sharing information that may be painful or even devastating. It's the *way* they share it that is key. These leaders state what they can, and let the folks know what they cannot share, and as a result, what they will do moving forward. These leaders take ownership of the information-sharing process and allow for ample questions.

This process fails when a leader shares information and then shuts down the questions. People process at different rates and speeds. Remember, if you have something tough to deliver, you have had time to process that information before it goes public. Your people have not. If you choose not to allow them to process it with you, have another resource available for them to do so. If you send them away after a tough information delivery, you send them to the depths of their own imaginations. They will process it...with everyone in the office that will listen, causing a magnitude 7.0 on the Richter scale in your workplace.

Here are the keys to delivering tough information:

1. Understand your goal – speak with the goal in mind.

2. Process through *your* emotions first, then go to your team.

3. Share openly what you can and cannot tell them.

4. Give them an option to ask questions and engage with you further; right there, or set a time before you adjourn when they can discuss it with you.

5. Give them a follow-up plan of what to expect and what is needed from them.

6. Check back in with them frequently in the days/weeks to follow.

7. Don't be afraid of your emotions. Even though you've processed them first, be vulnerable to allow others to see that you, too, are hurt, frustrated or bothered by the news.

This works for individuals and for teams. Communicating the good, bad and ugly is just something we *get* to do. As with most things in life, it's in the *doing* that creates the success or failure.

Moving from Breakdown to Breakthrough

Now that you know the three powerful words *help me understand*, and you have had the tough conversation about *what's next*, how do you continue moving the proverbial needle forward after some difficult encounters with your team? You keep revisiting all of the new learning points and communication points.

Remaining open with your team and available to them for questions is probably the biggest indicator of success here. However, I am not one to advocate for an "open door policy." In fact, I think it's something that sets everyone up for the greatest hurt in the office. I know, shocking right? I actually questioned this *norm* of cubicle nation!

In my last desk job, I had a director who was a fantastic leader. I probably learned the most from him about leading teams. When he took the position in our division, he showed up on his first day to give us the view from his chair in a bold way. He professed to everyone that he had an open door policy and was always available for us. We could bring our questions, frustrations and complaints about anything in the organization directly to him. He wanted to hear it all and help be a solution. He went as far as to say that if he wasn't in his office that anyone, at any level in the organization, could email him and he would respond same day. The culture that he walked into was *not* accustomed to this. So of course there were the naysayers from the get go, and many of those people tested the theory just to confirm it would fail. But there were also those that took him at his word, and for the first several months of his time in that position, it seemed to be working; at least until there were some major changes coming to the way we did business. His availability shifted, and the priorities of the day were sweeping through the office. Everyone knew big changes were coming and had concerns about how we would maneuver through it.

As his schedule increased and capacity decreased, people started to murmur and talk around the office. His door wasn't as '*open*' as it once was, and he wasn't getting back to people as quickly, if *at all*, when they emailed. The same individuals were consuming his time, and he backed off on his upfront communication with everyone. The shock waves were felt across the organization.

Sadly, there were people cheering that he had failed and couldn't be trusted, because he was giving all his time to a few individuals and somehow didn't care about the rest of the employees. Now, because I was on the inside, I knew that it was due to the fact the very individuals were problem-solving with him and addressing the needs of the whole organization to preserve jobs. But he didn't feel he could communicate that boldly, because he didn't want folks to shut down the work out of fear of getting a pink slip. His open-door policy worked against him. And what he did next is the reason that he is on the top of my list for exceptional leaders that know how to go from breakdown to breakthrough.

He shared at public town hall meetings around the state that there were things happening in the organization which would bring about big changes. He went on to say that while he does like to believe he has an open door, lately he hasn't due to the depth of information on his desk he was working through. He apologized and then gave them a new solution. He shared that, while it was his intent to be accessible, at times he could not due to the nature of the business. And that he wanted people to still bring their issues forward, it would just need to be through a new avenue. Ultimately, needs and concerns would get to him during this busy season, but not at first pass.

Then he asked for everyone on his team to hold him accountable to it. That was a brilliant move. And for someone reading this book, that brilliant move is *your* golden ticket.

Great leaders allow their team to hold them to the standards they have set and to be accountable for the work, people and goals in front of them. Exceptional leaders aren't afraid to fail in front of their people.

That director went from breakdown to break-through with his people at every level. He showed his real self, a vulnerable side, by admitting a fail point, and then gave them a new way of navigating and a new set of expectations. The bonus: everyone had permission to hold him to it.

Moving through the process took time but interestingly, in an organization that was riddled with negative Nellies who were hell-bent on seeing him fail, the performance of the whole organization increased. The efficacy in the office was palpable. It made this larger-than-life director seem human, while showing that he was not above reproach. Fear of failure was removed as he was willing to fail forward in front of his team to move everyone forward.

Questions to Ask Yourself About Communicating When You Don't Want to:

What do I fear about having this conversation?

What is my goal for the conversation?

How might my emotions get in the way? What can I do about that upfront?

On a scale of 1 (low) to 10 (high) how comfortable am I with being direct?

How am I showing personal accountability to my team?

What bold conversation do I need to have today to move my team forward tomorrow?

When have I seen direct communication work well?

What changes do I want to make in order to have direct conversations?

Who have I been avoiding in the office? What needs to happen for that to change?

How can I help my leader with accountability for myself and for my team?

What changes do I want and need to make in order to receive direct communication?

How might my behaviors and actions be setting up my leader to fail?

7

CONFLICT - IT HAPPENS

"Peace is not absence of conflict; it is the ability to handle conflict by peaceful means."
– Ronald Reagan

Far too often, I hear people say they would prefer to walk away from a situation to avoid conflict rather than face it head on. And on one hand, I don't totally disagree with them. But then there is always that second hand, isn't there?

For the demoralized team, nothing impacts and perpetuates feelings of *less than* and *not good enough* more than a culture of avoiding conflict. Reality is...*conflict happens*. How we learn to deal with it makes or breaks us as leaders and teams.

Each one of us has a default system for addressing conflict: some people become aggressive and others become passive. The valley in between those two personality types is like a black hole in outer-space just waiting to be discovered. It is our job as a member of the team, at every level, to press in to uncover the hidden truths.

If you have ever been on a volunteer board or team, you have seen the devastating effects of conflict avoidance. The team is in place simply to serve others, such as their church or their community, and yet somewhere in the hustle and bustle of volunteering serving each other has been forgotten. Non-profit organizations can be brought to their knees when conflict is present and not dealt with. Often this stems from lack of clarity on who is leading the effort, and when and where the buck stops. With whom, exactly, does it stop?

We should expect that our volunteers are serving only to improve the plight of others and for the mission of the organization. Sadly, most are serving to promote *self* over mission. Yes, that probably just upset some of you. But reflect for a moment on your last volunteer committee or that last auction or event you helped plan. Who on the team was truly there for the good of the cause and wore it like a badge of courage? Now, look around the room at the people you didn't trust or who avoided working. It may have been because of a hidden, personal agenda. If I was a betting woman, I would bet that the table is leaning on the side of *self-serving mission drift* as opposed to suspending oneself for the mission's success.

I see this in churches. I see this in community organizations. I see this in NFP's and fundraising efforts alike. The sabotage produced by conflict avoidance is not a respecter of persons, places, faiths, beliefs, or of great commissions. When working with people who work for free, we have a built-in mechanism that tells us our work matters more and *if it's meant to be, it's up to me.*' That, my friends, is why leaders of volunteer efforts have an incredibly high rate of turnover.

Retention for volunteer teams is difficult to define. Often lower expectations or standards are set for this kind of service, because after all, we are all *just* volunteering. Leaders of these teams may feel awkward placing high expectations on the people they serve with, so instead create a *'come as you are and when you want'* way of operating. For leaders, the thought of, "What if they quit?" becomes all-consuming.

Working with volunteers who see themselves as *'voluntolds'* can be daunting to say the least. Just because a group of people give of their time and energy to an organization, doesn't mean their values are in correct alignment with the work in front of them. When difficult situations arise, the individuals will often try to take on the solution themselves while not involving the other members of the team or organization. Throw conflict into the mix, and you will see adults put their heads down and take flight like a flock of sparrows who just took off from a field to avoid an attack. The irony is that with some groups of volunteers, the only harmony they reach *is* the conflict. Working with opposing agendas is a sure-fire approach to breakdown and failure. To avoid working through the conflict as it comes up is nothing more than accepting it as normal.

For our work teams, where everyone is financially compensated for their efforts, acceptance of conflict has a slightly different outcome: it keeps us chained to underperformance. You cannot thrive in a situation where you collectively avoid the *pink elephant* in the room. Every single member of the team has the responsibility to confront the situation. It is not the sole responsibility of the leader.

Avoidant behavior, whether at work, home or as a volunteer, attacks our personal power and self-efficacy. And in doing so, we tell others how we want to be treated. We show people what we value and what we fear. When trying to keep the peace, an environment is created and normalized where *conflict avoidance* is nothing more than *conflict acceptance*. Ultimately, this perpetuates the very behaviors and attitudes that are holding us back from achieving our goals.

The time is now! It's time to learn the valuable lesson about conflict. Know that you have the power to make choices when conflict arises. You can purposefully choose to resolve or avoid, and if you choose to avoid there can be real costs to you and others, both personally and professionally.

Conflict happens! Someone will steal your sand bucket or disagree on the blueprint for your castle.

When people work together, it's bound to occur. Unfortunately, many of us find it very difficult to face conflict. While conflict avoidance may seem the easier choice, I've seen it have long-term consequences...and they aren't pretty. So, why do so many of us avoid resolving conflict? Here are some reasons:

- I'm afraid others won't like me if I speak up.

- What if the other person says something worse about me?

- If I wait until I'm really angry, I may lose my temper...and so could they. When I've tried it before, things escalated or nothing changed.

- I am just too nice to get into confrontational situations.

- My skills and confidence needed to resolve conflict are lacking.

> *"People fear offending someone more than they fear pain."*

There are many costs of conflict avoidance. The greatest cost of all may be the cost to an organization as a whole. How often has someone come up to you and taken your valuable time to describe how frustrated they are with *Bill* or *Nancy* or how they wished he/she would change! When employees are having these chats, you can bet they aren't doing their work. Goals or profits can quickly take a back seat to conflict.

Also, there is a much more *human* cost of conflict avoidance. It impacts morale and energy when employees get frustrated and angry. Also, employees tend to internalize what they hear over and over again. If back-biting becomes the work culture's steady diet, it can often ruin not only your organization, but employee health! Conflict avoidance clearly hinders collaboration and teamwork. Employees aren't as creative, willing to take risks or to share new ideas. Some may also spend their time plotting how to *one up* someone else. What started as an easily manageable molehill can gain momentum and become overwhelming. In the end, everyone loses.

How can we prevent paying the price of conflict avoidance and instead reap the benefits of healthy employees working together in a productive environment?

• Accept conflict as a part of organization life. When people work together, there can often be conflict. It's what you *do* with and in the conflict that determines the results.

• Prepare employees for conflict. Invest in training and practice sessions ahead of time so employees will be ready and willing when it happens.

• Encourage employees to voice conflict and ask for help in resolving it. Conflict is often a key part of personal growth and development, resulting in improved employee and organization performance.

- Use a structured approach and common language to address conflict. Make it easy for employees to succeed by giving them the right tools.

Conflict and the Role Gender Plays

As a strong woman who does not shy away from sharing thoughts and insight, as you can imagine, I have been called many colorful names over the years. As I maneuvered my way through cubicle nation, I learned many lessons on the differences in gender and conflict in the workplace. As I observed other behaviors in the office, I noticed the stark contrast in the ways people communicate during difficult times. It wasn't always about the differences between men and women. Personally, I found it much easier to deal with a man if there was conflict in the workplace than I ever did with a woman. Men communicate differently than women and, in general, feel differently *about* conflict – it's just that way.

Communication is an element of everyday life. Conflict is created when people share different beliefs about a specific issue. Many factors shape personal beliefs, including gender. Gender can play an influential role in a person's opinions and, consequently, in their course of action.

Research suggests that males and females communicate using different styles of interaction. Men and women are biologically different, but evidence also demonstrates a social difference. The patterns displayed in cross-gender communication (communicating with the opposite sex) often reveals how men and women interact interpersonally. In conflict situations, contrasting behaviors and response differences between the sexes become more evident. There is a vast collection of research defining and explaining the differences which exist between males and females and how those differences develop within communication. Conflict is a prevalent element of all relationships. The manner in which it is handled is crucial to the survival of those relationships.

In the book, *Men are From Mars and Women are From Venus* (2004), John Gray wrote: *"Men mistakenly expect women to think, communicate, and react the way men do; women mistakenly expect men to feel, communicate, and respond the way women do. We have forgotten that men and women are supposed to be different. As a result, our relationships are filled with unnecessary friction and conflict."* (p.4)

This chapter is not designed to tell you how to be anything other than responsible for your own reactions, and to compel you to step up and confront the conflict you might be facing, even if it's uncomfortable. But to do that you must first understand your own default system and know the values that drive you. When people avoid confronting a challenging situation, no matter their gender, they do so out of fear and/or to protect their own interests. When you are working on a team, and the goal is to succeed *together* (remember the tide raises all ships), then our primary responsibility is to ensure that we are doing our part to co-create a healthy work environment.

Accepting the fact that conflict happens is one thing, but perpetuating the conflict by avoiding resolution to it is something completely different. It is imperative here that you don't get caught up on the word 'accept' when it comes to conflict. Our teams are littered with people who accept mediocrity and sub-par results in the workplace today. When I go in and dig deep into the culture of an organization, I can expose where the breakdown is happening and then support the company or organization in trying to see it for themselves.

A few years back, I had the pleasure of working with a group of elected officials in my home state. This was one of my favorite teams to work with, and even today the experience holds a special place in my memory book. At the same time, it was also the most difficult team to engage. Each individual had a clear agenda and was so entrenched in their private, workplace silo, that the only co-created expectation was one of conflict avoidance. The trickle down to the frontline workers was like a tsunami approaching shore. All appeared calm on the front until, "Here it comes!" The tsunami hit: someone's agenda was compromised or sabotaged. The casualties to the staff were far–reaching, while the team of leaders for the organization turned a blind eye and put a tick mark down for their silo (or licked their wounds).

One elected official in particular seemed to be at the core of almost every problem this organization had. He played in the sandbox much like the neighborhood bully with no exception to person or position. His lack of attention to the very people that had committed to a lifetime career serving the people of their county, showed nothing but disrespect.

As an example, he only made himself present for the meetings where *his* agenda items were being discussed. The down line of people that he lead within the organization were flying blind most of the time until he showed up to tell them he didn't like them or the work they did. Unfortunately, this was a rather frequent occurrence. The other members of his elected team were simply trying to get through the term with him, hoping he would not do insurmountable damage in the meantime. The relationship was so bad that even his counterparts would walk down the hallway and turn the other direction if they saw him coming.

His aggressive manner was palpable to all, and he didn't care one way or the other who (in the office) saw it. His public demeanor, however, was quite different. This position was clearly a stepping stone to something bigger on his radar.

During one of our leadership coaching sessions, we were talking about what it meant to lead your people. We were outlining the guiding statements for the organization and doing our very best to align with a cohesive positioning statement of who we wanted to be seen and celebrated as, as an organization. When it came to discussing how to lead the teams to success across the board, he blurted out the sentiment in his heart that he had been modeling all along: *"Tammy, you keep calling us leaders of others, what makes you think I am a leader? I am not here to lead people."* After I recovered from the *'did he just say that?'* reaction going off in my head like fireworks, I asked him what he meant exactly.

He went on to say that he did not take the job to lead people. He was here to move his constituents' agenda forward, and that was all. Then he re-stated the fact that he didn't see himself as a leader.

Interestingly, this guy who showed up every day to do nothing more than just get by, while bullying people in the process, just showed his *hand* to the group. He had no idea, training or capacity for the job that was before him, and his outbursts were rooted in fear of being exposed.

What this elected official didn't realize when he said yes to putting his name on the ballot, was he also said yes to leading people. He had a large staff that hung their hat on this career. They were proud of the work they did every day, and they deserved to be lead or released to do the job they knew how to do. His bullying approach and micromanaging when it was good for the public profile to do so was not empowering the workforce.

When he appeared frustrated with the people around him, it was nothing more than being fearful of being exposed as not good enough. In that breakdown, we had an incredible conversation from the whole group about the value of the staff that were the *boots on the ground* to getting the work of the county done. By the end of that session, we had shed a little light on the truth about leading as an elected official, and his team rallied to help him create a new picture of what his job could look like.

At this breakpoint, communication opened up and conflict was no longer accepted as the norm. They began to work differently together, and while some of the relationships were never fully repaired, as a unit they could agree on the common goal of supporting the people that worked for them to be the best they could be.

That official was in office for only one term. He realized, in pretty short order, he was not cut out to lead in this capacity. It was not why he ran for office in the first place. His picture of what his life and career would be like did not match the reality of the job he was appointed to. So he wisely self-selected into another opportunity outside the realm of being an elected official.

Sometimes we even avoid the conflict inside our own self and react from that inner conflict out of protection and fear. The best solution every time is to get real with yourself and understand what you are avoiding. Ask yourself, "What am I avoiding and why? What do I want to change about it?"

As I told this elected official, I also hope you hear these important words:

> *Your people are in their jobs because they want to make a difference, first. They are waiting for you to lead them. The reality is they will outlast you and may even outwit and outplay you during your tenure as their leader. But at the end of the day, all they really want is for you to step up and lead.*

Questions to Ask Yourself

What is your relationship with conflict?

How do you most commonly avoid conflict?

What success measures do you have in place to address conflict?

On a scale of 1 (low) to 10 (high) to what degree do you see conflict in the workplace?

When have you accepted conflict as normal?

What impact is conflict avoidance having on your team?

What one thing can you change today so that you can address conflict tomorrow?

What are you avoiding at work and why?

Who are you avoiding at work and why?

When have you had success confronting a difficult situation at work?

How might you approach conflict differently as a result now?

8

STAND FOR CHANGE

"You must be the change you wish to see in the world." – Mahatma Gandhi

The only consistent thing I can hang my hat on in organizations today is *change*. If there is one simple truth about the world, it is that change happens, and it's how we adjust to it that matters most. That is not an earth-shattering statement to make, and I'm confident you will agree with me on it. So then, if change is constant, the question is why do we fight against it so much?

In spite of popular ads and slogans, the world doesn't change *one person at a time*. It changes as networks of relationships form; small groups of people who share a common cause and vision of what's possible. This is good news for those of us who want to change our organization! We don't need to convince large numbers of people to change. Instead, we need to connect with a few like-minded people.

A corporate coaching client who wanted to increase the capacity of his team called me to discuss a situation at work. "We had to reduce expenses within the company, so I made some changes in the organizational structure of the department by consolidating a few positions, putting several projects on hold, canceling one project, and letting a few people go," he explained. "I didn't think it would be any big deal, but some employees in the department are acting like I'm as ruthless as Attila the Hun. Several are avoiding me, and a few have become downright hostile in their attitude towards me. I don't understand why they're acting this way."

Leadership is about leading, but it's also about considering the human factor in implementing changes, as my client found out. While many people like to joke that the only constant in business is change, change has an interesting way of affecting people that can often result in resistance. This resistance can range from fairly subtle reactions, such as avoidance or passive-aggressive behavior, all the way to outright defiance, hostility and sabotage.

What is the best way to avoid resistance to change? Seek to uncover potential resistance *prior* to implementing change. Determine the way you will address the resistance from the start.

What my client didn't realize is that he wasn't just a

manager; he was also an implementer of change within the department. According to Rosabeth Moss Kanter, Professor of Business Administration at Harvard Business School, "The best tool for leaders of change is to understand the predictable, universal sources of resistance in each situation and then strategize around them."

Prior to making changes that will affect others, it's important for managers to carefully think through:

- what the specific changes include,
- who the changes will impact,
- how it will impact them, and
- how they might react (understanding reasons why people might resist the changes).

Knowing this information makes it easier to create a plan of action so changes can implement smoothly.

Let's take a look at the important questions for this process, and use my client's situation as an example:

What the specific changes include: In this case, the changes involved re-structuring the department, consolidating numerous positions, laying off several employees, canceling one project, and putting several other projects on hold. Not *small* changes, indeed!

Who the changes will impact: Mainly the department employees, but the changes could also impact other stakeholder groups if any of the projects cancelled or put on hold include cross-functional team members from other departments.

How the changes will impact them: The biggest impact is to the employees being laid off. They will experience both an emotional and financial impact. Employees whose jobs will change could also have emotional and financial implications, although to a lesser extent. Employees' job tasks will change for those whose projects were put on hold or cancelled. Finally, there will be an emotional impact to everyone in the department, whether or not they are directly affected by the changes.

After analyzing this information, the next step is to look at what I've found are the five main reasons people resist change:

1. Fear of the unknown/surprise: This type of resistance occurs mainly when change is implemented without alerting the affected stakeholders *before* the change occurs. When change (especially what is perceived as negative change) is pushed onto people without giving them adequate warning and without helping them through the process of understanding what the change includes and how their jobs/work will be affected, it can cause people to push back against the change, due to their fear of the unknown.

2. Mistrust: If the individuals in a department highly

respect their manager because the manager has built up trust over a period of time, the team will be more accepting of any changes. If the manager has not proven themselves trustworthy in the past or is new and has not yet earned the trust of their employees (like my client), then mistrust can manifest itself into resistance to change.

3. Loss of job security/control: This type of resistance often occurs when companies announce they will be restructuring or downsizing. This causes fear among employees that they will lose their jobs or be moved into other positions without their input.

4. Bad timing: As the old saying goes, "Timing is everything." Heaping too much change on employees over a short period of time can cause resistance. If change is not implemented at the right time or with the right level of tact or empathy, a smooth transition won't be realized.

5. An individual's predisposition toward change: Differences exist in people's overall tolerance for change. Some people enjoy change because it provides them with an opportunity to learn new things and grow personally and professionally. Others abhor change because they prefer a set routine. These are usually the people who become suspicious of change and are more likely to resist.

Bottom Line:
Take the time *before implementing* to understand: 1) what the specific changes include, 2) who the

changes will impact, 3) how it will impact them, and 4) why they might resist the changes.

Being aware of the reasons people resist change will help you implement change with fewer issues along the way. Eliminate fear of the unknown by letting affected groups know there will be changes coming. Avoid mistrust and the feeling of loss of control by getting others involved in the changes before they occur, asking them to offer feedback. Prevent bad timing by providing a clear vision and reason for the changes, along with a timetable or schedule of what to expect and when to expect it.

Standing for and implementing change is never painless, but it can be a lot less painful for everyone when it is done with empathy and compassion after thorough analysis, planning and strategizing.

What happens when you are afraid of the outcome of a change? A small business client of mine was preparing to make significant changes to the way they serve their customers. After an in-depth look into their business and industry standards that were typical for running the type of business they owned, they came to the conclusion that they wanted to stand out from the crowd. To do this would require completely redesigning the way they ran their business *and* going against the industry norm.

After careful contemplation, we looked at how

their team would be impacted, but even more carefully at how customers would be affected. During one of our coaching sessions, we discussed their fears around how their customers would view the change. To increase their capacity for growth in their business, they needed to adjust the way they offered their services. The risk for them was not knowing whether their customers would like the change or not, and if not, they would ultimately take their business elsewhere. The fear of loss of revenue was great, but the power of possibility was greater.

The two business owners co-created a strategy to make the desired transformation to their business model, which included a communication plan for their customers; something they would launch prior to the changes taking place. Additionally, they worked through their fear of losing revenue by getting a solid vision of what they were moving to with the new approach.

Together they agreed to stop waffling on what might or might not happen, and keep their attention focused on the goal of growing their already successful business to new heights. They held strategic conversations and events within their community to unveil the changes and to highlight the positives of what it meant for their customers.

Had these clients backed off the vision they had for the company's growth at any point in time, they would have likely failed before they started.

Keeping your customer in focus when you embark on change in your company is imperative. Building a solid plan, complete with a communication strategy, is paramount to your success as you stand in the threshold of change.

Empower Leaders to Lead

A close sister to change is empowerment. For companies wanting to implement vast change, or even small tune-ups, step one is releasing their leaders to lead the people through it. Far too often, I see a top-down decision from corporate headquarters that institutes a change to the organization with either little to no direction on the 'how' for their leaders. Or in other cases, the how-to is so magnificently detailed, they are impossible to follow. Somewhere in the middle, between micro and macro-management, is empowerment. It's the team sweet spot; that spot when the team lands on it, their capacity increases and efficacy soars like nothing else.

Remember, your people want autonomy at work. They want to make a difference. By restricting the leaders' ability to move their team forward through change is ultimately limiting your own capacity. When our leaders are empowered to lead, their teams will follow. If you shackle a leader by micro-management or by disallowing creativity, you tie yourself to a disempowered and demoralized crew that is likely to look for their next promotion *outside* of your organization.

Empowerment means creating an environment where people are equipped and encouraged to make decisions in autonomous ways, and to feel that they are in control of the outcomes for which they are responsible. It means opening the door for dissent, avoiding groupthink and encouraging innovation.

To understand some of the complexities of this type of empowerment, we will be looking at it from the perspectives of leaders and employees. Empowerment involves distributing authority throughout the organization. The leader's perspective is where it all starts. What does empowerment mean for the CEO and management?

Empowerment from the Leader's Perspective

Empowered leaders behave in an empowering manner, by: (1) influencing through context, (2) creating a culture of inclusion, (3) giving and not taking back control, (4) providing moral and logistical support, (5) communicating a clear mandate, and (6) equipping people for success.

Influence through context implies trust in a higher principle or guiding force and belief in the creative potential of human nature. It is a matter of trusting the process. It is not *giving power*, but creating a context where empowerment is released and nurtured. Leaders define the context and standard at every level by giving people freedom to act and innovate, thereby developing leadership and producing proactive employees, giving them a competitive edge.

Create a feeling of inclusion to nurture and empower. Develop an atmosphere of inclusion across all levels, making sure everyone has a voice, and ensuring their voices are heard. Leaders welcome dissent as a source of objectivity and innovation. New ideas must be allowed in the decision-making process to generate solutions superior to those achieved through the exercise of positional power.

Give up control and do not reclaim it. Expect to go through a phase where managers are faced with ambiguities and a sense that things are out of control. During this uncomfortable phase, it is tempting to tighten the controls again. Resist the temptation to tighten control if you want your people to use a proactive approach to problem solving. Once responsibility is given, do not try to take it back.

Articulate the common purpose. Do not mistake empowerment for an absence of direction. The leader needs to create the vision and clarify goals. A lack of clarity about desired outcomes and role expectations is disempowering. Being accountable to *specific* expectations is better than not knowing where you stand. It is critical for the leader to clearly define the common purpose, goals and limitations. If not, employees will be hesitant. Pass the ball and let the associate run with it—but run within the ball field. Stay inbounds.

Responsibility for, and commitment to, a clearly articulated mission is essential.

Equip people for success to insure the best chance of success. This involves training, resources and information. Too often, employees are given responsibility for which they are not equipped. This brings the feeling of entrapment. Consider setting up an unallocated resource pool for solving unforeseen problems. Leaders provide their people with all the information they need by making information readily available to people at all levels through more channels.

Empowerment from the Employee's Perspective

To experience empowerment, employees need to develop skills in and practice: (1) open communication, (2) work in teams, (3) critical listening, (4) tolerance of uncertainty, (5) resilience and courage, and (6) accepting responsibility.

Open communication is a willingness to put our thoughts on the table; to be exposed to scrutiny; to own up to one's ideas, assumptions, biases and fears; and helping others do the same. Corporate cultures that promote creativity are characterized by direct interaction and openness—a climate where ideas are owned and challenged through honest dialogue. It may not be comfortable, but it is a necessary condition of empowerment. Such openness cannot be coerced.

Willingness and know-how for working in teams is

essential. It is not just self-empowerment. It is a collective change that comes by learning respect for the contributions of others. Empowerment is not a win-lose paradigm where an increase in the power of one results in a decrease in the power of others. In MMC's Team Building course, participants learn to value the uniqueness of the other players. By discovering and emphasizing the gifts of each individual, the experience of empowerment increases for everyone on the team. Utilize every unique, creative tool you have in your sandbox!

Gain wisdom to be fully empowered. To move from dependence on superiors for decisions, one must move beyond what they see and the knowledge of the way *it's always been done*' to make appropriate decisions. Wisdom is the result of thinking about the future, recognizing trends and anticipating events or outcomes that may affect the organization, and from interactions with customers, suppliers and others with whom employees interface directly.

Tolerate uncertainty. Empowerment can be threatening. Expect some employees to resist empowerment. This is especially true when not only the outcomes, but when the means, methods and ways have always been clearly defined for them by others. Decisions about how to get things done, when left to the employee, can be disquieting for the leader. This uncertainty is a change from working in an established routine where employees adhere to set rules and procedures.

Under pressure, employees tend to run to the leader seeking resolution and closure. Leaders who do not understand the dynamics of empowerment, out of misdirected compassion or because it makes them feel more powerful, often succumb to these requests by telling them what to do. This is disempowering and reestablishes dependence.

If employees are encouraged to think for themselves, goals and boundaries need to be clearly defined. This establishes guidelines for use of intuition and thinking across departments and disciplines for solutions related to their common purpose.

Resilience and courage come from within. The source of a person's confidence is not in others, but in one's own inner strength. Empowerment means to be forward thinking enough to live with mistakes and failures without being impaired. Those living with self-doubt will be unlikely to accept the challenge of empowerment because, for them, more responsibility means more chance of failure. Every failure threatens their sense of self-worth. Empowerment is very personal. Acceptance of higher levels of responsibility is inherent in an empowering context.

Accept responsibility for outcomes. Empowerment goes beyond delegation, and encompasses the burden of responsibility. Empowerment must be balanced by responsibility. They cannot blame upper management, suppliers, other department heads, or anyone else for failure to produce desired results. This enables them to learn from their mistakes. Empowered employees are willing to have their performance measured by objective written assessments because these are opportunities for feedback and improvement. Part of responsibility happens when you see inappropriate management conduct or receive inappropriate direction. It's important to have all incidents documented and to save them in a safe place.

Teams develop when individuals move outside themselves and become concerned with the success of all other members. This means that employees become concerned, not only with the success of their immediate responsibility, but also with the success of other members on the team. The group then becomes a unit where the development of one member increases the power of the team.

Alignment with a common purpose is a must. To empower people in an unaligned organization can be counterproductive. If people do not share a common vision and do not share common goals, empowering people will increase organizational stress and make it impossible to maintain coherence and direction. An organizational commitment to empowerment would be foolish if leaders did not share the same vision and goals. To create an empowered organization, you must structure processes, goals, people, and reward systems to align with each other.

There is a direct relationship between empowerment and organizational vitality. It is about the probability of change, of keeping up in a changing world. People learn best when they see a relationship between their life and the concepts being taught. Without sensing an organizational commitment to fully implement empowerment, these concepts will be very difficult to implement. Only when people have authorization to dissent with the leader do new ideas have a chance to surface.

Questions to Ask Yourself

How do I stand for change?

What are my personal feelings about change?

On a scale of 1 (low) to 10 (high) how comfortable am I with change?

When have I succeeded in the face of great change? What did that feel like?

When have I failed to make a necessary change? What was the outcome?

How am I at motivating others on my team for change?

How does empowerment show up on my team?

Do I feel empowered to truly lead my people or myself?

What are the common goals for my team? How effective are we at moving toward them?

How well does our team support one another and lift each other up?

What did my last assessment reveal to me about my level of empowerment and comfort with change?

How do I see myself as an agent for change on the team?

9

BREAKING OUT

"If you think you can do a thing or think you can't do a thing, you're right." – Henry Ford

Now that we have opened up our minds' eye to change, defined the rules of the sandbox and looked at empowering behaviors in ourselves and others, let's go a little deeper. It's time to take off the gloves and get to the truth of the matter—why you do the job you do. I want to grab the nearest shovel and start scooping up the past failures, let downs, successes and hurts to look at what lies beneath. Because if not now, when?

Office buildings today are tightly planned spaces where about 40 million North Americans [source: Newsham] go, day after day. They are filled with fake, 5 foot tall walls covered in cheap, dust-collecting fabric that makes my eyes itch and offer no privacy. The office air is repurposed throughout the building, and if you have access to a window, consider yourself lucky. Day after day, people everywhere wake up at ridiculous hours and put themselves through long, dangerous commutes, all to sit in a 6' x 6' box for eight or nine hours. If this is the plight of the American worker today, who wouldn't want to break out? Unless, maybe, someone finds cubicle nation comforting?

Okay, a little dramatic? Perhaps. But if this is the environment that we have relinquished our professional selves to, shouldn't we do our ever-living best to make it a happy place? Isn't it our responsibility to improve the environment just simply by being in it? Over the years of working within the confines of a cubicle, and now returning as a consultant to work with demoralized teams—most of whom feel stuck without an escape hatch—I have seen the effects that *one* attitude can have on the whole office. This attitude can have either a negative or positive impact.

We have co-created a powerful toxicity in the work environment, with the other cubicle residents that can have life-altering effects on our whole system; the system of work and the system of life. So why do so many choose to dwell here? What keeps us coming back for more?

Today, I put the stake in the ground to combat this attitude: '*lack of knowing what we really want and a loss of dreaming for more.*' We have turned our job environments into '*have-to*' rather than '*want-to*' situations.

Several years ago, I had the wonderful experience

of returning to a state agency office similar to the one I left over a decade ago. In fact, a few staff members there were people I had worked with during my time in state government. Much to my disappointment, little had changed. And that was exactly why I was there. It was a great opportunity to work with this team on defining what a healthy culture looks like and strategizing with them to build one.

This was no easy task: it required me to do some intense introspective work on my own past attitudes and beliefs around working in a cubicle, day in and day out. But thankfully, as I did my own work, it brilliantly transferred out to others: I embarked on a mission to transform the way these people looked at their jobs, each other and their cubicles.

Do you know how much potential you have? Do you know how much the average person uses on a daily basis? Well the answer may shock you so try to avoid shutting down from it or rejecting it, mentally. Here it is:

You have unlimited potential!

You truly do! However, if you are like most, you only use between 7% and 10% of it on a daily basis. Yes, only 7% to 10% out of 100%.

Somewhere in the 'just get through the day' world, we let go of pressing toward and accessing our full potential. Instead, we have settled for something far less, as we sit by collecting our bi-weekly paychecks. Many of us are not even able to identify what makes us happy anymore. We can, however, identify other feelings: an overwhelming feeling of numbness, emptiness, and for some, a burning rage and feeling of powerlessness.

Worse yet, workers struggle with loneliness. I have heard loneliness is one of the largest emotional problems Americans face today, even in offices when co-workers are just inches away on the other side of the 5' padded wall. A severe loss of direction in life demoralizes a person, and that's difficult to shake off.

Today, when I observe and address the culture within a team or organization, we start by taking a look at the drivers behind fulfilling our potential. We do this by defining our values as individuals and of our team. Next, we cross check them to see how they align with, or oppose, one another.

Why do I start here? Without a defined set of core values, which every human being has internally, we cannot set our sights on moving toward what we really want in life. Knowing our values opens us up to what's possible for our lives and future. Without clarity, we aren't able to understand what triggers our reactions to different stimuli. When it comes to team values clarification, it is necessary to understand where your team and organization places motivations.

If you are not working from your core values,

you are not working from your place of truth.

Let me pause...you might be thinking I am setting up this chapter with a big push to leave your job and break out of cubicle nation. That could not be further from the truth. As most people learn in relationship breakups, you can't take the baggage from one bad relationship into the next and expect to be successful. Jobs are no different. Each individual must clean up their own mind, assumptions and wounds before moving on to any other opportunity. If you elect not to, the problems will simply follow you around and only the geography will change. The focus of this body of work is to help you create an awareness about your environment, the people within it and to understand yourself and what drives you.

To identify what motivates you and the people on your team, it helps to look at these four areas of behavior:

Habits: these are the daily habits that either hold us back or propel us forward. They are the things we do every day without even realizing it, because we are so *'routinized'* in the way we go about our business.

Attitudes: the attitudes we have about ourselves and others. Attitude moves us toward our work or away from it. This includes how we see our own success in our current position.

Beliefs: beliefs create the image and self-talk we

have about ourselves. Beliefs are often not talked about when it comes to work, because our leaders and our teams get into a position of *'just do it'* rather than understanding *why* someone does what they do.

Expectations: we hold expectations about everything and everyone. These are often the greatest fail points in relationships, too, because each individual often retains unspoken expectations that can *never* be met unless they are communicated.

Your Habits, Attitudes, Beliefs and Expectations (H.A.B.E.'s) are the four main drivers for *potential*. If you struggle with any one of the 4, you will limit your potential. The only way to move the boulder up the towering hill called *Your Potential*, is to get the strength and stamina for the push.

Start by looking at your habits. If you aren't getting where you want to go, investigate the *why* by looking at the daily routine you keep. Open up to the idea that perhaps your habits are part of the problem. Change won't happen unless you decide to work it out. When you work out for exercise, you build up muscles by lifting a weight, repeatedly. Building a good set of habits is done very much the same way, with repetition. Identify the habits that limit you right now, and open up your mind to new creativity.

The next step in the process is to check in on attitudes you hold about yourself and the people around you. If there is someone in your office that you are avoiding, that behavior stems from an attitude you hold about that person. If your team isn't performing at the level you want or need, ask them some powerful questions to expose underlying attitudes. When we do this, we expose the belief system cemented into their minds and hearts. Our beliefs are the source where we get the momentum to stay the same or make a change.

Here are three powerful questions to ask yourself:

What do I believe to be true about my current situation?
Is it really true?
Or is it my *opinion* of the truth?

Asking yourself those questions starts to crack the code on habits, attitudes and beliefs. Taking time to investigate those three sets you up for success before you go after tackling your expectations. I believe that by addressing the first three, before you move on to unearthing expectations, is what gives you optimal success. It also helps unearth any underlying disgruntled attitude you have been holding onto. If we go straight to expectations with our people, we can come across as offensive and judgmental; each of which are counter-productive to the goal.

Breaking out of old patterns has the potential to transform the way you view your work if you allow it to. Holding on to patterns that do not serve you is a choice; a choice that says, "I decide to stay stuck exactly where I am."

Many years ago, I led a team effort where I worked that involved bringing people from all over the state to one centralized meeting spot, and we would be meeting several months in a row. I did not have the luxury of handpicking every person on the team: it was about 50/50 - my boss also wanted to have input about who participated. Our task was to coordinate and deliver a multi-day, organization-wide training conference in one central location. Seems easy, right? At times it was...at other times...not so much.

There was one person on the team I was carpooling with to our monthly meetings. Our discomfort with one another was palpable, to say the least. She felt that *she* should have been given the position of lead on the team. I can see how it made sense in her mind: her role within the agency *was* that of a training coordinator, but here I was appointed to lead this large endeavor, simply because of my previous experience planning large events. Even so, I was chosen. It wasn't my call, nor was it hers.

In all transparency, I didn't see the value she brought to this endeavor, and perceived her to possess a negative attitude about everything and everyone. Her glass wasn't even *half* full.

To top it off, our values could not have been more different. There had been an overt criticism of my every word, thought and action long before we were placed on this team together. You know the saying, "keep your friends close and your enemies closer?" Well if this team was going to be successful, we needed to do our part to keep the naysayers in a quiet calm. This co-worker was the loudest one, and she also had an exceptional amount of influence.

Working with this person was probably one of the greatest challenges in my professional career. She pushed *every one* of my buttons, and I know I did the same for her. To make matters worse, this attitude was bleeding into the rest of the team. Because of the unresolved issues the two of us had, we were affecting the whole team and creating a toxic environment.

Just as the planning was picking up momentum, our organization was advised that some big changes were coming, and positions were going to be taken away. It wasn't long before I heard the news that this woman was included in a major reduction-in-force effort by the state. She would lose her position with us and be moved off to another agency.

On one of our road trips to a planning meeting, she broke down in tears in the car, laid everything out on the line and exposed herself to me at a very emotional level. I always love conversations that start with, *"You know I don't like you...but..."* We took the long route there so we had extra time to talk about what she was facing. It was important for me to listen to this very panicked, fear-filled woman discuss her anger toward me and the organization. Yet despite her anger, she didn't want to leave her position.

On that car ride I learned a very important lesson. Judging someone because of an expectation about their beliefs, work habits and attitudes would make me just as bad. She talked about her fear of losing momentum in her career. She viewed me as attacking her ability to be successful because of my position leading the event team. I recognized that I was not actually the problem.

Her beliefs, both personal and professional, were nothing more than a contrast in values and a different way to express them in the world. We both held a high judgment of the other person based on our beliefs and attitudes. Our habits and the way we had become accustomed to interacting were not only affecting us, they were now impacting a team; a team trying their best and giving their time to coordinate a major project.

We each had placed very unhealthy expectations on one another. I had an expectation that she was trying to sabotage, and she had an expectation that I wanted her to lose her job. Neither could've been farther from the truth. We had created a toxic environment for everyone else as well. It took this crossroad – the unknown future and the present vulnerability – to expose the core of what was going on.

This colleague reached out to me. The one person she *admittedly* couldn't stand. The reason? Ironically she saw something in me she needed that day: she found me to be a very confident person who was good at helping people see opportunities before them, and knew I was a praying woman. And, while she was a self-professed Atheist, she felt I was the one to come to for help and comfort in a time of deep need.

It was my opportunity to step up, suspend judgment and be different with her. I needed to let go of my need to be right. That exchange shifted my view of her, and by doing so, it adjusted my attitude.

Our values would *never* be in alignment. That was not the goal. But now that I had more understanding of *her* value system, I could choose to show up differently with every encounter. Sometimes, the people we work with aren't meant to be our friends. But it is our responsibility to be considerate of the rest of the team, and not allow personal feelings to affect the team's ability to be successful in the workplace.

In order to change the way we view a person, we must investigate core beliefs. If we choose not to, we may be creating the toxic environment that we spend eight to nine hours a day working in.

There is one last point I'd like to share regarding belief systems. Just because *we* change a habit, attitude, belief or expectation does not mean others around us will. Case in point, my colleague's view of me did not change once that crisis was over. I had hoped it would, but that choice wasn't mine to make. She returned to the comfort of locking onto her fear and discontent, chumming up again with two bedfellows that she had counted on in the past. For me, it only exposed more of what I knew to be true:

You cannot change the people around you, but you can choose how you play in the sandbox with them.

"Breaking out" doesn't exactly mean we break out of the work place. We *break free* from the chains that have us bound to a lackluster or less than joyous environment. We loose the things that bind us to old patterns of belief, unmet expectations, attitudes or habits that may be crippling us—from anything that keeps us from walking in our full potential. If you truly want to increase your potential, start by expanding your awareness of your H.A.B.E.'s.

What happens if leaving the workplace *is* the next best step? What if you, like I did, find yourself with a perpetual bruise on your forehead because of running into the same wall again and again? Even the padded cubicle walls leave a mark when you bounce off them enough times!

So how do you handle that thought? First, go back to unearthing your values and your H.A.B.E.'s about *self* and the environment you work in.

Understand *why* things are not working well for you, or *why* you feel change is the only way to make it better. Sometimes just getting clarity in these areas is enough to formulate a new plan for remaining content in your current environment. Other times a bigger shift is required.

You don't need to make this decision in a silo—do not go it alone. Pull in your trusted advisors, the people that are truth tellers in your life. Wise counsel always sees things you don't. Ask for their input, not from a place of negativity or to push you to make a change, but from a place of objectivity. Everyone needs a person in their life that can be 100% objective, so that you can formulate the next best step while cleaning up your own baggage.

Hold on to this truth: leaving your current team with bags packed full of disappointments, wounds and frustrations only sets you up to take old attitudes, beliefs and expectations with you to the next cubicle. It won't take long before you find yourself feeling broke, busted and disgusted there too.

"For some, when it's time to leave a job can be quite clear—whereas for others, it might not be so obvious," says Ryan Kahn, a career coach, founder of The Hired Group, star of MTV's Hired and author of *Hired! The Guide for the Recent Grad.*

Employees know when they've reached a point where it's time for a change, because they find themselves reflecting (on a regular basis) upon whether or not their job aligns with their long-term goals. If the two are not aligned, they often make adjustments to keep things on track. As for others, they don't realize they're unhappy with their job until someone points it out to them, or they realize they spend too much time being unhappy about their position. It's the topic that keeps them up at night thinking, *what should I do?* They consult with friends and family, seeking advice to validate their reasoning. They know the answer, which always involves change, but the difficult part is making the change itself.

Here are seven signs a change is eminent:

1. You are miserable every morning and dread getting up to go back to *that* cubicle.

2. You discover you really don't like working with the people around you and can't avoid facing it any longer.

3. You're constantly stressed, negative or unhappy at work.

4. Your work-related stress is affecting your personal health.

5. You don't fit in with the corporate culture and you no longer believe in, or align with, the company's mission.

6. You are bored and stagnant in your job.

7. You are experiencing verbal abuse, sexual harassment or are aware of any other type of illegal behavior.

Once you realize it might be time to leave your job, you'll first want to set goals for yourself detailing what you are looking for in future opportunities in terms of responsibilities, company culture, compensation, and benefits. Next, think over timelines for yourself for finding another opportunity and making your exit. Then, write it out! Create your transition *game plan* complete with timelines and objectives.

Finally, don't let emotions cloud your decision making or get in the way of making a critical decision: look at it purely from a business perspective. Know the compelling *why* to leave or to stay. And whatever you decide, be willing to do your own personal work to ensure that you are healthier when you leave than you were when you came in the door. When you transition out, never burn bridges. In today's world, people and things are well-connected; more than ever. Make a point to always be professional and accept your responsibilities every step of the way.

Questions to ask yourself

What Habits might be in my way of reaching my full potential?

What Attitudes might be in my way of reaching my full potential?

What Beliefs might be in my way of reaching my full potential?

What Expectations might be in my way of reaching my full potential?

How might my H.A.B.E.'s be impacting the way I play in the sandbox with my team?

What values drive me? (Visit the resource section for a values assessment)

10

SO, YOU HAVE AN UNDERPERFORMER

"Never has it been so important to field a team with the best players. Every smart idea matters. Every ounce of passion makes a difference."
– Jack Welch

As a manager, maybe one of the most difficult situations you may encounter in your career is dealing with underperforming employees. How you respond, react, act and handle them can determine whether a problem is quickly resolved or becomes an even larger issue. In the sandbox, the underperformer affects more than just their leader; they dramatically affect the success of the team as a whole.

Underperformers – the word itself shows they are performers who don't meet expectations. They definitely can be brought up to the desired category – the *performers*. For that to be initiated, the human resources office or their immediate supervisor should have a direct, open communication with the individual. Once the competency of the worker/team member is understood, the situation can be addressed in a thoughtful manner.

Performance impacts the goals of not just the individual, but also the entire team. Low performers can be *formed* due to many issues in the organization including communication, unclear goals and targets, ill-defined expectations, as well as the H.A.B.E.'s we talked about in the last chapter. Although the issue may not be caused by the systems in the organization, it can also be due to the nature of the individual.

The quick way to handle this is to get rid of the underperformers, but is this the best way to handle them? You must ask yourself, "Is this one person truly the root of the problem, over–all, or are we hanging our pain on them?" Too many times I have seen people labeled as the team or unit's 'problem' be released quickly from their position, yet the true problems remain.

Not ALL underperformers are the root of the issue for you and your team.

Performance is evaluated by comparing it with underperformance. If underperformers do not exist, performance has no existence. It seems to be our yard stick for measuring the whole team. Underperformance also changes from context to context, e.g., *somebody's junk may be somebody else's treasure.*

Do not ignore underperformers. Consider changing your vision to see talents in them, nurture them and get results. Be cautious about identifying temporary underperformance and then labeling that person as an underperformer. You may fail to identify the potential in that person that could unleash great possibility for the team.

If you don't respond in a manner that supports your future, you run the risk of losing a top employee in your organization. Weighing the to-do's and don't-do's with your underperformance issue takes an especially accurate scale of measure.

I have had the pleasure of hearing many stories about underperformance, managing people *forward* and rules of engagement in the sandbox. While collecting stories and experiences for this book project, there is one story that stands out. It's the story of Cliff, an upper-level manager with a very specialized set of skills in a highly-technical industry. Several times, Cliff applied for a promotion to become a director in his business unit. Each time, he was passed over with little or no explanation from his boss. The odd part was that each time he put his name in the ring for the promotion, he was encouraged to do so by his boss and corporate execs alike. Yet, each time he was passed by, and the position went to a newer member of the team; one was a person with fewer accounts, and another was a person who was on corrective action the year prior to their promotion.

When Cliff inquired as to why he continued to be passed over, there were several reasons from the director. "I can't lose you from the position you are in," was one, and another was the all-too-often excuse, "You don't have experience leading people." Finally, out of sheer frustration and a feeling that he had hit the proverbial glass ceiling, Cliff left the company and went to a competitor in this specialized industry to gain management skills. His hope was to return to his original company and to the client work he loved, but secure an upper-management position.

A time came when Cliff was pursued by his former employer to return, with the promise of promotion. He was put under the same leadership within his former team. Though the personnel terrain had changed dramatically in his absence and several others had left, his direct superior was still there. When he reached out to the others to ask why they left, they said it was because he wasn't there to help guide the projects and the director was not leading them well.

Cliff's hypothesis had been confirmed. The issue was not that he or anyone on the team didn't have the right set of skills; they were all skilled. Cliff had been doing the job of the director as he motivated and led people throughout the office on their projects. While that wasn't in his job description, he knew that was best for the team and clients. His heart was motivated by doing whatever he could to move his team forward. So upon returning, he had a new perspective, a great bump in pay, and a new level of responsibility given by the CEO. Cliff was soon to realize that his return did not bode well with his immediate superior.

If you haven't realized it all ready, Cliff was working for an underperformer who rode on the coattails of his team and their talents to promote *himself* forward. The director, whom Cliff was reporting to yet again, could build the widget, but didn't know how to build the people. As Cliff supported the team in achieving their goals, targets and measures, the director took the credit for himself. He criticized Cliff's work to the corporate executives, which is why he repeatedly had been previously passed over for promotion. The director realized that if Cliff promoted, he would lose the leader of the team and the one with the greatest talent and ability. It would ultimately affect the way he, the director, would look in corporate's eyes.

This is actually a classic case of how to create a demoralized team: when someone takes all the credit for the work of the team, they hold back and put down the top performer, keep them hidden in the barracks of the work team, and hold their purse strings tightly. Cliff found that while he had the ear of corporate for the work he did, there was something present in the relationship with his boss and the corporate leadership that kept this underperforming director in a position of power. It was a mystery, but something (or someone) kept him there despite his ineffectiveness.

Ultimately, Cliff found out that the system wasn't going to change, so again, he needed to leave. Being stifled, even in his new position, was killing him on the inside. Completing the clean-up of the mess created during his absence was not motivating him to stay any longer. Cliff also knew that his personal attitude toward his direct superior was one riddled with lack of respect and expanding frustration. The situation was not likely to change because there was no opening for dialogue around the problems. The team could not reach their full potential under this form of leadership, clients were being impacted negatively and he no longer had the stamina to be the fix-it man.

Cliff made a decision that supported his values. He pressed for change by attempting to open up conversations with decision makers about the problems, but sadly they viewed him as the fix for the clients, and neglected to create a fix for the organization. You see, sometimes our corporate leaders get so focused on the customers, end-users and clients that they neglect to tackle the root staffing problems. The business case for the team was to address the underperformance of the leader, but the easiest solution for the client was to have their star performer, in this case Cliff, working all their accounts. One has to wonder, if they did a business review of the situation as it pertained to time-loss, hiring costs and new hire training, all due to the poor leadership, would they have made a different decision?

If you have an underperformance issue with *any* member of your team, I recommend running the numbers to see the fiscal impact over all. Being short-sighted by calculating only what's coming in can deplete you greatly because of what's going out in man-power costs.

What to Do When You Find an Underperformer

While dismissal may be your sole option in extreme cases, most of the time you can turn around an individual's job performance with the right approach and the right attitude. What's important is to implement a fair system that matches the consequences to the action. Assessing the situation from the people side *and* the financial side is key. Here are steps to take to address underperformance issues.

- Take immediate action.

- Don't wait until an employee's formal review to discuss poor performance on the job. Remember, before someone can change, they must know what they're doing wrong.

- Schedule a private meeting to talk about the issue and be as specific as possible.

- Make sure the employee is provided with the opportunity to respond to your concerns. There may be issues you're not aware of, like pressures at home or problems with co-workers, which might be adding to the problem.

- Make notes during all conversations.

- Provide clear direction.

- Create a plan for improvement.

- Make sure that your own actions don't send a conflicting message.

- Do not go overboard while providing encouragement.

- Assign a mentor. Select a mentor who possesses strong interpersonal skills and an enthusiastic attitude.

- Monitor the situation.

- Make sure to praise when an employee does achieve objectives, even minor milestones.

Often, minor changes can lead to dramatic improvements. Stay committed to your goal. You may find that a below average or underperformer is able to change into a productive employee with only a few minor adjustments. However, it will require that you as the leader have the stamina to follow through impeccably well to course-correct for you and your team.

Don't forget the team. When you have an underperformer on your team, and you are spending one third of your time addressing the issues, you can't afford to stifle your team in the process. This is where transparency is of utmost importance. No, you don't tell your whole team what is happening and why. But, you do affirm the good and let them know you hear their complaints. I recommend you also ask them what they need to see happen before they feel that the problem is being remedied. Why? Because in the sandbox, we can't hide out. To make it all work, we all must feel we're part of the solution.

When it comes to adding people to the sandbox, your hiring practices are the key to your success. One of my favorite expressions is 'slow to hire, quick to fire' and I encourage my clients to take that very literally. Too often, I see hiring choices made around people that we like and secondary is their ability to perform. When my clients have chosen new employees based on the 'like factor,' they often end up spending more on training and development just to get them up to the level required to perform the basic duties.

We fall in and out of 'like' with people all the time. And when performance is measured by targets and goals, a very tangible element, we find quickly that we can't measure the like factor objectively. However, we hold onto people because we like them with no business case to back it up. That is dangerous.

<u>The 5 P's of a productive team:</u>
Proper
People
Placement
Prevents
Problems

The primary goal when adding to your team is to identify your underperformer before you hire them. To do that, you must fight hard against the three main hiring impulses that most often get managers into trouble.

The first is using your *gut*. Don't do it! When you have a job opening to fill, it's just too easy to fall in love with a shiny new candidate who is on his or her best behavior, telling you exactly what you want to hear and looking like the answer to all your prayers. That's why it's important to never hire alone. Make sure a team objectively analyzes the candidate's credentials and conducts interviews. And by all means, make sure the team includes at least one real tough cookie; the kind of naysayer who is particularly good at assessing the job fit and sniffing out the fakes.

The second instinct you have to fight is what Jack Welch calls the "recommendation reflex," in which managers rationalize away negative references with excuses like: "Well, our job is different. They'll do better here." You should seek out your own references to call, not just the ones provided by the candidate, and force yourself to listen to what they have to tell you even if it ruins the pretty picture you are painting in your head.

Finally, fight the impulse to do all the talking. In other words, ask and button down your urge to talk. Yes, you want to sell your job, but not at all costs. In interviews, ask candidates about their last job, and then keep quiet for a good, long while. As they describe what they liked and what they didn't, you will likely hear much of what you really need to know about fit. And further, always, always tie it back to the objectives to avoid becoming personally invested in the person. That is the most costly mistake as noted with the story about Cliff.

The corporate leaders were emotionally invested in the underperformer as well as the clients and not invested in the success of the team as a whole. It polluted the sandbox and ultimately caused a ripple effect that prompted clients to take their business elsewhere.

How fast should you move when you sense you've made a hiring mistake? In a word: *very*. So fast, in fact, that if you're moving at the right speed in taking care of a hiring mistake, it will probably feel too fast. That's okay. In every case, a rapid intervention is better for the organization, your own career and even for the person you're letting go.

Questions to Ask Yourself:

Do you have an underperformer on your team?

How would you know if you had an underperformer on your team?

When have you been a member of a team with an underperformer in the sandbox?

How much time do you feel you work with underperformance on your team?

How much time can you afford to give to an underperformance issue on a daily basis?

What support do you need to tackle the performance issues on your team?

What bold conversation might you be avoiding with an underperforming team member?

From your perspective, as a team member, who's responsible for addressing underperformance?

On a scale of 1 (low) to 10 (high) what is your level of comfort with addressing underperformance in your organization?

What 3 resources do you have to support you with tackling underperformance for you or your team?

11

IS YOUR PROBLEM CAPACITY OR COMPLEXITY?

"Complexity keeps many successful leaders focused on the present and sometimes the past, instead of thinking about the future, where all growth and progress lie." – Dan Sullivan

How to keep your team steadily improving is the million dollar question for leaders today. It requires an evolving system of development concepts and growth strategies that will enable any success-seeking individual to acquire the capabilities – and achieve the results – of the very best leaders.

As we face the changes of an ever-changing business world, we realize that it is important to continuously increase our capacity for more. To do so, we must break through the ceiling of complexity. It is absolutely necessary for the survival of an organization.

So what *is* the ceiling of complexity?

We know that all the growth in a person's life occurs in stages. Within each stage, the individual comes to a point where it is not possible to base further growth upon his or her existing knowledge and skills: this means the individual has reached a ceiling of complexity. Sometimes this ceiling is permanent, which is why many people fail to grow beyond a particular stage of development.

For a team, it can look a lot like *exhaustion of capacity*. It might show up in conversations like *'do more with less.'* It may also be the element that is promoting behaviors that are consistent with underperformance issues. Or perhaps you realize that your systems are not performing as you need them to. Simply put, your people may not be able to see beyond what is currently in front of them to achieve the desired results for you. Try as you might to inspire and motivate them, if they can't see it, they won't achieve it. And no matter the system you have in place, people trump that every time.

To best dig into the issues of capacity vs. complexity we need to first go back to what a highly-functioning team looks like.

What are some of the characteristics of a team functioning at the highest level of excellence?

1. **Clear, elevating goal:** Team goals need to be very clear so that everyone can tell if the

performance objective has been realized. The goal needs to be involving or motivating so that the members believe it to be worthwhile and important.

2. **Results-driven structure:** Teams need to find the best structure to accomplish their goals. All teams need to have clear roles for group members, a good communication system, methods to diagnose individual performance, and an emphasis on fact-based judgments.

3. **Competent team members:** Groups should be composed of the right number and mix of members to accomplish all the tasks of the group. Members need to be provided with sufficient information, education and training to become (or to remain) competent members. This is where *slow to hire, quick to fire* may just come in handy. I am not advocating for firing everyone at the first sign of difficulty, but I want to bring awareness that when we hold on to people beyond their expiration date, it tears at the fabric of a team.

4. **Unified commitment:** Teams do not just *happen;* they need to be carefully designed, fostered and developed. Your people will work for you because they trust you first, and that comes by fostering open dialogue and autonomy.

5. **Collaborative climate:** Trust based on honesty, openness, consistency and respect seems to be essential for building a collaborative climate in

which members can stay problem focused, be open with one another, listen to each other, feel free to take risks, and be willing to take a stand for one another.

6. **Standards of excellence:** Effective group norms are very important for group functioning. The standards need to be clear and concrete, and all team members need to be required to perform to standard. (No backsliding here because we 'like' someone better than another.)

7. **External support:** High-functioning teams need money, equipment and supplies to accomplish goals. Reward the work on difficult team assignments in terms of raises or bonuses for that performance. Acknowledge success measures along the way. Remember the autonomy component. Your people are coming to make a difference, not necessarily for the carrot you are dangling.

8. **Principled leadership:** Effective team leadership is a central driver of team effectiveness, influencing the team through four sets of processes: *cognitive* (understand the problems confronting the team); *motivational* (helps the team become cohesive and capable by setting high performance standards and helping the group to achieve them); *effective* (handle stressful circumstances by providing clear goals, assignments and strategies while being transparent about the process); and

coordination (matching members' skills to roles, providing clear performance strategies, monitoring feedback, and adapting to environmental changes).

It's time to ask yourself, of those characteristics, what do you and your team do well? Where is the greatest area of improvement? When we can talk from that perspective, we can then start identifying how to build our capacity. If all areas are a 10 on your scale of measure, and that is the top, then you as the leader must look at yourself to inquire what it is that you really want and need from the team.

You see, helping people navigate through cubicle nation is often helping them to see what *they* offer and what *you* value. If our capacity is exhausted and our systems are flawed, then what? If everyone is truly firing on all cylinders and we still aren't hitting the goal, it's time to ask some very tough questions about the work ahead. The feeling of overwhelm can quickly derail a team, even a great team. It's up to every single member to keep their own emotions in check. It is the responsibility of the leader to empower their people to make decisions from truth versus fiction. It is crucial to have the proper system in place to identify the performance traps we can set for ourselves.

How to Build Capacity and Teams

Every step in the innovation process is an

opportunity to build capacity and teams. I believe that 80% of all desired knowledge, skills, attitudes and behavior are already available in most organizations. The trick is to unleash this potential. I have run many workshops where participants surprised each other (and themselves) with the useful experience and abilities they had to help the organization move forward. But had the conversation not happened, we would never have known it.

Here are five tried and true action items that you can employ today to have a capacity reality check with your team:

1. Don't look at what employees need to learn, but what they can teach.
You may be surprised at their knowledge.

2. Work from questions, not from answers.
When change is the topic of conversation, it's tempting to answer all questions you can immediately. From your perspective, your overview may be better than that of the members of your team, and answers provide security. Questions, however, tell much more about what is really going on in people and by exploring them and having people answer their own questions, you get much further.

3. Have people participate and interact.
Knowledge is not best transmitted one-directionally and attitudes and behaviors are not learned by listening. Create a safe space

with expectation of full participation. To do this, it's best to co-create rules of engagement with the team from the start. I begin that exercise by asking this question, "What do we each need today in order to feel that we can fully participate?"

4. Build (on) experience.

Change can be so incredibly scary that even the most beautiful framework is not enough to comfort people. Positive experiences can, though, even if they stem from a virtual situation and another time. In a good session, ideas are put to semi-realistic action so people build hands-on experience with the change that is needed. On top of that, they learn to work together in new situations and can build on each other's knowledge.

5. Set action items and takeaways.

Too often we go to meetings or open up group dialogue with no clear objective for an outcome. Be the voice for what 'we do as a result' in every conversation you have. When people feel that they actually accomplished something at your meetings and that there is accountability and follow-up as a result, their level of participation will increase.

Urge and Enthusiasm

As we discussed last chapter, the very first step in any process is to get the right people on board and make them enthusiastic and ambitious enough so they *want* to start moving. Urge and enthusiasm is about feeling the need to change and *wanting* to change as well. All this happens before there's even a sense of where change should take you and what you will do. Urge and enthusiasm is the basis of any successful project.

Obviously creating a shared sense of urgency or enthusiasm does not work by *ordering it* top-down.

Where bold conversations are encouraged, I have seen consistent team dialogue used as a successful tool to stimulate people's sense of urgency and enthusiasm. I believe empowered employees are more than capable of discovering what's urgent and what's not. Enthusiasm is a byproduct of growing a more knowledgeable and cohesive team climate. The sandbox is about collaboration, trust and enthusiasm for creating.

Every member of the structure has a role to play to ensure that the core value of the team is being fully realized. It's not enough to simply show a TED talk in a meeting, combined with interactive exercises to align everyone's attitudes in the sandbox. True teamwork happens when building capacity involves creating opportunities for bold conversations; a safe space for team members to discuss truth, experiment and make mistakes. Hosting a short series of lunch meetings can be enough to get a team back on track and moving towards success, temporarily. However, one-hit wonders are a one-time deal and not sustainable sources of enthusiasm.

I worked with a team where the leaders in the organization decided they would host bi-weekly brown bag lunches and run them as open Q&A time. This was the employees' opportunity to bring their questions, concerns and ideas to the table for safe discussion. While this was a great idea, one that I even promoted as a way of creating trust and open dialogue in the organization, it was going to require great consistency from leadership. Sadly, their enthusiasm waned, and ultimately the lunch room was filled with zero leadership and just frontline team members. You might imagine what type of conversations were taking place then.

When you want to promote change, growth and/or increase in your people and do it as a unified front, you must be 100% committed to seeing it through. If you are not, you will cause greater harm than never having flipped that switch at all.

It takes time and dedication to build capacity and teams, as you no doubt have noticed. Turning ideas about the future into everyday action is not a walk in the park.

Once you have the high-performing team you want and all parties are playing well in the sandbox, how do you sustain the momentum? Because like it or not, at the end of the day, we can't just stay at the same level. The world around us is changing too quickly. That competitor you've had your eye on has just been bypassed by the one you missed and you must move quickly. That is where your *systems* of complexity for the work come into greater focus.

The systems you have for operating must remain in constant criticism; criticism of whether or not they support growth potential or limit you to current level capacity. A new state of simplicity is required. No further progress is possible because the existing stage of growth is filled with the complexity of experience—the messes, stuff, details, complications, conflicts, and contradictions that come from doing things a certain way for a long time. One thing immediately becomes clear: working harder and longer in the existing stage no longer works. In fact, it becomes counter-productive.

New concepts and strategies are needed to achieve a new state of simplicity. The new simplicity of thinking, communicating and performing enables individuals to break through the ceiling. When we choose the future over the past, we enter a new stage of growth: we break through the ceiling.

The ceiling of complexity is a fact of life for everyone, everywhere. Individuals, groups, organizations, industries, and countries all run into the ceiling of complexity. Global society is running into ceilings—overpopulation, starvation, pollution, terrorism. All current stages of growth in all areas of human activity eventually coalesce into new ceilings.

Learning how to break through the ceiling of complexity, therefore, is perhaps the most important life skill that any individual can develop. And when fully developed, new leaders are born in that moment to take evolving teams forward. But it all starts in one place: taking a very thorough look at individual capacity, drive, urge and enthusiasm. It requires reflecting on the person in the mirror and asking the question, "What do I need right now?"

As you have noticed throughout every chapter in this book, we have reflected back to one main ingredient, one baseline, one common denominator—Y.O.U. Whether you are a member of a team, leader of a team or CEO of the company, change comes when you explore it for yourself first. Growth happens when you expand your own personal vantage point and increase your self-awareness. At that point, the systems you have in place can change.

Capacity and ceiling of complexity are very individually focused, then and only then can we expand outside to look at the team as a whole.

Questions to Ask Yourself:

Have I reached capacity in my current role?

What systems do I have that support growth for the future?

Where have I stopped reaching inward in order to grow outward?

If my team is not high performing, what is the root? Capacity or complexity?

What systems do we need to develop in order to expand?

What does my team say about capacity and complexity?

What resources can I call upon to lend a critical eye to my systems?

On a scale of 1 (low) to 10 (high) how unified are the members of the team?

What one change can I make today to expand my capacity tomorrow?

12

PUTTING IT ALL TOGETHER

"At the end of the day, your Why must be bigger than your But." – Tammy Redmon

I find myself pausing as I come to this last chapter of *Sandbox*. There is still so much that I want to share with you about team work, leading a team and leading the most prized possession—you! But alas, it's time to put all the pieces together and wrap up this part of your journey.

My hope is that this book will be used as a tool in today's adult version of the sandbox: cubicle nation. I also want to see you pull new insight and powerful questions from it and gain new understanding about how your team works.

We have covered a great deal of information in the previous 11 chapters. Together we have revisited the rules of the sandbox (that we all learned as children) and how, while many years removed from playing in one, the rules are very much the same today in the workplace. We took a bold look at the demoralized team and how each of us impact its success or perpetuate its problems. And we exposed some truths about our habits, attitudes, beliefs and expectations that either limit our potential or expose new opportunities. But nothing is as important, in my mind, than gaining the tools and courage to have bold conversations with our teams, with our leaders and with ourselves. If we can't have truth telling conversations with one another, we do nothing more than put shackles around our ankles, tying us to our excuses and bad behavior.

You see, the sandbox today is *your* place to make a difference. It is *your* place to design the future for yourself that you truly want. No more limiting beliefs or excuses about what's possible. If you learned just one thing from *Playing in the Sandbox*, I hope it was the realization that your future success depends upon your ability to know your *why*, accept responsibility for the things you can change and have bold curiosity to take a stand for things that seem impossible.

Today's teams are built of people just like you and me; people who want to know their work matters and live a life of meaning. To do that, we must refuse to allow excuses to remain as we live between the padded walls of cubicle nation. Our responsibility is to know *why* we do what we do, *why* we work where we work and *why* we matter. The *Why* must be bigger than the *But*. That means the heart and drive that propel you to get up and go into the office every day must be bigger than any excuse that comes your way. Stop settling for *'just get by'* or *'because we've always done it this way'*—go back to the sandbox and create!

Create a new picture of what you want your days to be filled with. If you're on a team where you feel pressed down, shaken around or held back, start the conversation for change. Or if you lead a team of lackluster individuals that you didn't pick in the first place, sit with them and co-create a vision together of how you want to play in the sandbox. Have that bold conversation. Design the cause that you can *all* champion. Or if the tides of change have put your team through the ringer, be willing to bring in help to open up the dialogue around the pain. Don't allow the ever-evolving business climate to keep you from exposing the collective potential of your team. Be relentless.

If not now, *when?* If not you, *who?* Change won't happen until we acknowledge the problem, expose it at the root and get our shovel, bucket, rake and water to start transforming, crafting and shaping our future.

Success is near: it may be only the distance between you and the mirror. Look in the mirror and start asking yourself some tough questions. Look deeply, and ask yourself if you have what it takes to get where you want and need to go. If you don't like your current job situation, hire a coach to ask you even tougher questions. Refuse to settle for anything but your *why!*

You've heard me mention the old saying, 'If it's meant to be, it's up to me.' I believe this only applies to your *why*. You are the only person who knows the *why* behind what you do and you alone can create the plan to go after it. As a member of a team, however, there is always a 'we.' 'Me' is just the upside down version of 'we.' Most things that get upside down, fail.

Think of the home loan debacle of recent years: upside down is not the right side to be on. Are you catching my point here? *Playing in the Sandbox* and navigating the currents of cubicle nation in today's marketplace requires that *you know you:* do *your* work first and become acutely, emotionally aware of you. That part is your responsibility. No one – not your boss, your team, your peers or your organization can do the work for you. Only you allow excuses to cloud your vision or distort your *why*.

Knowing beyond the shadow of a doubt *why* you do the work you do – from a heart centered, values approach – unlocks a new found freedom. I know this to be true. Our *why* and our values are not a respecter of persons or positions. They are the glue that holds each individual together in the workplace or they are the time bomb about to run out of time.

Throughout the book I've mentioned a common thread: values. Now is the time to bring "values work" into high-definition color for you. It is the very work that propelled me to leave a job I loved and a career I was deeply committed to for a greater purpose. When I was faced with the decision to leave my cubicle behind because of feeling demoralized and frustrated, three words made my decision crystal clear. I stared at these three words on my paper:

Family. Integrity. Self-Respect.

I had discovered my core values; the very values that were in complete contrast to the values of the organization I pledged my allegiance to. There was no bridging the gap between the core of my being and the core of the organization. It made my decision easy.

Before knowing my core values, I stumbled around my purpose and tried desperately to understand why I was there. I was fighting to make a difference and ran into wall after wall the harder I fought. Truly I believed that I was in that place to tell the good, bad and ugly as I promoted the cause and good work our organization did in the community. And yet it wasn't working. You see, my *why* then was tied to other people. And when I got clear on my core values, I realized that was out of order. Our *why* must be tied to our heart, and our values are at the very center of it all.

Whatever your position is today, I invite you to look at what is at the center of it all for you. Do you know the core values that drive you each and every day? I am not talking about what you *think* you know...you must know beyond the shadow of a doubt what drives you, motivates you, moves you, and compels you to be you in the world.

How do you know what your core values are? Aside from doing the introspective work to identify them, you probably know them because they are the very things that cause the growing bruise on your forehead (as they did for me). You know them when someone presses against them: they cause a fight-or-flight response when pushed upon. They become evident because of the emotional reaction when someone or something pokes at them. When touched, passion is evoked from the center of your being.

Everyone's set of core values is like the navigation system in cars. Core values are the GPS for our life. So if you are off course with where you thought you'd be or where you feel called to be, then it's time to align your values and get back on the road you are meant to be on. But I caution you – don't attempt the journey without first gaining the wisdom of your core values.

To make this easier for you, I have included a values assessment link in the resource section of the book. Visit the link and use this tool today. Take the time to discover your core drivers. Go one step further and have your team take the assessment, too. Knowing the values that propel them to be who they are in the world will help you have those bold conversations and align with your team.

Some of the healthiest teams I have seen engage with one another from their values proposition. Knowing what values drive your people as individuals gives you new tools to use when working through the challenges that you will face.

The success of your team depends upon them knowing their *why*, honoring their values and communicating with one another respectfully and clearly. The 50/50 rule of communication discussed in chapter 5 becomes *much* easier to apply when we know our values and when our *why* is bigger than our *but*. When personal values are clear, we create less finger-pointing and blaming, while promoting more collaboration and connection.

As you dig into some of the workplace challenges you face, you have been given many new tools to try on. When I say *try*, I'm inviting you to use them with an open mind, believing that they will work, and if not, then try a different one. Pick one place to start and give it all you've got. Look at the clarity of the targets and measures you have set with your team. Are they clear? Do they clearly understand them and their plan for achieving them? Get in agreement. Do an internal audit of yourself as a leader, and ask your team about the areas you do well in and where you can improve. Next, do your work to improve.

One Senior VP that I worked with had a Leadership 360° evaluation completed by his boss, peers and direct reports. The results were challenging for him to look at because it felt so very personal. But there it was...in black and white...he couldn't argue with the differences in how he rated himself as a leader and how others rated him. The standard of deviation on the report in some areas was pretty large. It was like a hot poker to his heart for him to look at. The question he asked himself became, "Are these areas places I can and want to make changes in?" From there he became open to coaching around the issues he may or may not want to change.

The report caused pressure for him. He realized the people he spent so much time with day after day clearly didn't know his heart and drive for doing his job; at least he thought that based on how he *perceived* their responses. Through coaching him regarding the results, we talked over options and a lot about behaviors and perceptions. This VP was compelled to understand more clearly the view from his colleagues' chairs and committed to helping them understand his view. But, had he not walked this process through with a coach, he would not have survived it: the emotional triggers were so strong.

I share that to say this: getting a power partner on your side to help you safely uncover the areas for change is critical to weathering through the pain points. You may be able to build the widget with perfection, but that may not be enough to be fully successful in your job. That underperformer on your team may be great at doing their job tasks, but may be costing you a great deal of time and resources with their destructive behavior toward the rest of the team. Stepping outside the tough situation you face and enlisting the help of a neutral party to help you see it clearly can be the single best investment you make toward building that high-performing team you most want.

Be bold and be willing to ask for help. The scotoma (blind spot) you may have about your team or your work will only get bigger until you bring in someone to expose it. Many of the tools offered in this book can be that *someone*. However – and that is a big HOWEVER – do your own work *first* to gain clarity and the data which supports it. Taking action to change someone else, when you and/or they are in an emotionally charged place, will be like a tidal wave making landfall in your team, having the opposite impact you want.

So in the end, it's time to ask yourself some very tough questions to assess what the right next best step is for you to take. After you have answers, create an action plan for taking the steps. I have made this process very easy for you. Simply go to the resources section of the book and go to the link for *Action Plan*, print it off and get started writing out your plan. Writing it down and making it clear with the *what, by whom, by when, why,* on the page will help keep you focused on the goal, especially if emotions are present.

Earlier I said that the statement *'if it's meant to be it's up to me'* applies most to *your why* (not a team's), and this is also true: *if change is going to be, it is up to me.* We are the ones with the power and authority to change ourselves in order to move toward our *why*. We can change ourselves in order to thrive in any environment we find ourselves playing in.

May your journey toward change expose the power of possibility and the beautiful tapestry of the life you want to create.

Questions to Ask Yourself:

What do I see as the greatest challenge in my current situation?

What have I tried to do about it?

Who have I enlisted for help?

What do I understand my 'why' to be?

What excuses have I used or am I using that keep me from my 'why?'

When have I blamed someone else for my current situation?

Who is ultimately responsible for my current situation?

What are my core values? How do I know these to be true?

How do my core values align with the values of the team I am on?

What are the core values of my organization?

How do our values align or collide?

When have I felt my core values pressed upon? What was the outcome?

If I had a magic wand, what would I change in my current situation?

If money were not a factor, what would I do with my career?

On a scale of 1 (low) to 10 (high) how comfortable am I with asking for help?

Who can I align with as a power partner for change? **Will they challenge me?**

What scares me about looking at my 'why?' Ask, 'What else?' to this question until you run out of things to add to your list.

What motivates me to change?

What is my greatest learning point from the Sandbox?

What one thing will I do differently as a result of reading Playing in the Sandbox?

Who will I share this book with to support their change effort?

ACKNOWLEDGMENTS

The next time I write a book, I think I will start with the acknowledgments first! I have a lot to say about a lot of things, but now at the end of this journey, I find myself a little out of breath. And surprisingly, out of words. Now I get to put down – for time and eternity – my astounding appreciation for the people that helped pull me through the sandbox. My prayer is that I do it justice. My goal is to keep it simple.

Who	**What**
El Shaddai	For Your endless love and abounding grace
My Kids	For the gifts to me that you are – I love you
My Former Employers	For giving me great material to write and teach about
My Former Leaders	For allowing me to learn so much
My Clients	For your grace through the writing process and for allowing me to be your coach, I am honored.
Mom and Dad	For loving me
Tracy	For being more than a sister, being my friend
Rusty and Ginny	For the Cottage, my safe haven to rest and restore
Krista and Debbie	For holding my hand through the publishing process
Maura	For making my branding and cover sing to me
Liz	For encouraging me to write more
Pastor Ray	For asking really great and powerful questions

Danielle	For your ability to make me laugh at myself (in public), and for reminding me never to settle
Pastor Dave	For modeling your heart for growing leaders
Pastor Dwayne	For your covering and your friendship
Vicki	For challenging me to go for what I want
Patrick	For standing with me and helping me find my true north
Kate	For cheering the loudest
Nan	For telling me to email Dan Pink!
Nikki	For being a bold truth teller in my life
My Church Family	For your love, support and endless encouragement
Mr. Shaudney	For throwing Hefty Markers at me in 4th grade inspiring me to ask more questions
Dan Pink	For your endorsement and inspiration
Bob Burg	For sharing your process of writing a book, *Costco Dogs and Bubble Gum*
The Reader	For saying yes to the book and starting your journey

RESOURCES

Helpful leadership plans and assessment links from Tammy's website:

www.theteamoptimizer.com/actionplan
www.theteamoptimizer.com/values-assessment
www.theteamoptimizer.com/team-assessment

Emotional Awareness Quiz

Copyright © 2003 Donna Earl. Used with permission.

Below are the behavioral habits of emotional intelligence. As you read these, rate yourself on the frequency of each habit or behavior.

I have this habit or behavior:

Always = 5 points
Usually = 4 points
Sometimes = 3 points
Seldom = 2 points
Almost Never = 1 points

Behavioral habits

1. In all circumstances, I respect other people and their feelings.
2. I can easily identify my feelings.
3. I take responsibility for my own emotions.
4. I can maintain control of my emotions.

5. I find it easy to validate others' feelings and values.
6. I do not rush to judge or label other people and situations.
7. I do not try to manipulate, criticize, blame or overpower others.
8. I constantly challenge my habitual responses, and am willing to try considered alternatives.
9. I live in the present, learn from experiences, and do not carry negative feelings forward.

My Overall Score = _____

Scoring Results:

40-45 =
High level of emotional maturity, awareness and control. You have a positive and inspiring impact on others.

35-39 =
Higher than average level of emotional intelligence. Concentrate on self-awareness and control, and developing increased empathy for others.

27-34 =
You have a base-line awareness of what emotional intelligence is. Be alert for opportunities to increase levels of self-awareness and empathy toward others, and to refine responses.

9-26 =
Now that you're aware of emotional intelligence, monitor your emotions and their impact on you and others. Notice how your behavior impacts others and get feedback on how to modify behavior which has negative effect.

How to ask powerful questions

In today's world of leading people to high performance, we are finding it is less about having the right answers, and more about having the right *questions*. If you are going to be a successful leader, learn how to ask good questions. Here are seven tips for taking this skill to the next level.

1. **Ask open-ended questions.** Questions that can be answered "yes" or "no" are closed-ended questions. They don't generate discussion and rarely yield any insight. By asking open-ended questions, you get far more interesting insights. For example, instead of asking, "Are you happy with your results?" you might ask, "Why do you think you got the results you did?" The first question can only be answered "yes" or "no." The second question invites reflection and starts a discussion.

2. **Get behind the assumptions.** Every business decision is based on assumptions. If you don't understand these assumptions, you may make a bad decision. It's helpful to ask yourself first (then your colleagues), "What are we assuming in this scenario?" Then, keep peeling the layers off the onion until you get comfortable with the assumptions. This exercise can keep you from making mistakes. The logic may be impeccable, but if it's built on faulty assumptions, you'll end up with a faulty conclusion.

3. **Get both sides of the story.** It's easy to hear one side of the story, act on the information, and then be embarrassed when you find out that you only had *half* the facts. I'm sure I have done this myself

hundreds of times. Now, I constantly remind myself, *there are at least two sides to every story.*

4. **Ask follow-up questions.** Avoid the temptation to comment on every question. Sometimes I like to see how many questions I can ask in a row without commenting. It's amazing what you can learn when you do this. Your comments or decisions will be much more informed. Often you won't get to the core issue until you've gone several questions deep.

5. **Get comfortable with "dead air."** Most people get uncomfortable when things get quiet. They feel the obligation to fill the space with chatter. Let this work to your advantage by just keeping your lips locked and your ears open. When you do, you will often find that people volunteer amazing amounts of information that you would have never obtained any other way.

6. **Help people discover their own insights.** One of the best ways to mentor others is to *ask* rather than *tell.* Yes, you can pontificate to your subordinates, but your insights will not be as meaningful to them as they are to you. You can accomplish far more by leading them with good questions. One of my favorite, especially in the wake of a mistake or disappointment, is this: "What can we learn from this experience that might be useful to us in the future?"

7. **Understand the difference between facts and speculation.** One of my former bosses once told me, "Make sure you tell me what you know and what you *think* you know, and make sure I know the difference." People make all kinds of statements that they think are based on facts. These should

immediately cause your radar to go off. Often you will have to ask, "Do you know that to be a fact?" If so, "How do you know?" or "Can you provide me with the source for that statistic or claim?"

Finally, when you ask questions, take notes. It communicates tremendous respect for the person you are interviewing. It is also very helpful when things get quiet. You can go back over your notes and discover new questions you haven't yet thought about or asked.

(Excerpts taken from http://michaelhyatt.com)

How to Have a Bold Conversation

Having bold conversations is important in the workplace. Instead of sweeping them under the rug, we need them to come up! Trying to get around them will ultimately cause breakdown in the fabric of our teams—something we all want to avoid!

People ask me how I start a bold conversation. Today I'm sharing my strategy with you. Here is my 5-point system for having a bold conversation:

Point 1: Get Clear on the Why. Take time to understand why you are reacting or feel the need to address something with boldness. Work through the emotions that are triggering you before you engage in a conversation that may also be charged with emotion. When you know the *why* behind the conversation at the start, and have worked through your emotions attached to it, you are half way to a successful outcome.

Point 2: Consider your Timing. Often when my clients have bold conversations with their teams, they eagerly start pelting people in the office with their new, bold tool. Unfortunately, timing in this case is everything. We need to ensure that the recipient of the bold conversation is in a space and place where they can receive from you. Select a neutral location and set it for a mellow time when there is not a lot of other activity, hysteria or pressure around the office. Ensure that our people are not pressed by other priorities either, as that may impact the outcome of the conversation. I suggest asking to schedule the time to talk and even giving the topic in advance so that no one is caught off guard.

Point 3: Lay the Foundation. When you are ready for the bold conversation and it's time to meet, it's your job to set the baseline of what you want to cover. Let the parties involved (an individual or team) know why you are meeting with them and what you are going to address. Avoid sugar coating anything. Let them know right up front that you want to have a bold conversation about something that is impacting the team, you, the office, etc. Invite them to participate by asking them questions (refer to the tips on asking powerful questions), and allow the person or people to have their reactions. If you shut them down, then you have taken your bold conversation to a bullied conversation. By laying the foundation of what you want to talk to them about, you increase your chance of getting to completion and resolution.

Note: *A bold conversation is not your opportunity to purge all your frustrations and concerns; it is a thoughtful dialogue to clear the air, gain understanding and move the team forward in truth.*

Point 4: Co-Create the Outcome. When you have given the outline or exposed the challenge to the team or individual, launch your best question starting with, "Help me understand ___." From there, design the action plan or outcome you're committing to together as a result. As an example, if you are working with a dysfunctional employee who is wreaking havoc on the office with their badgering outbursts to co-workers, you want to understand whether they realize the impact they are having. You want to understand if they would like to be treated in that manner. You want them to stop the behavior. However, telling them how wrong they are for their behavior and demanding they stop is not a bold conversation: conversations are two-sided. It's your job to enroll them in the success of an outcome that changes their behavior.

Point 5: Follow-Up. After you have a bold conversation with your people or a member of your team, follow up with them in short order. Check in to see how they are doing and to thank them for having the dialogue with you. Affirm and acknowledge the decisions and outcomes that you co-created and ask if there is anything more they need from you. If this is a peer-to-peer conversation, it is just as important to follow up on. We want to keep our conversations moving forward in the future. Sometimes people go away from an exchange, meditate on it and get upset. By having check-ins after the initial conversation, it helps diffuse pain and/or open up new dialogue based on the new reaction. Always go back to your *why*: it is the beacon guiding the ship to shore.

ABOUT THE AUTHOR

Since 2003, Tammy Redmon has been helping leaders who are frustrated with their dysfunctional teams, take the group they have and transform them into the team they want!

Praised as a "Secret Weapon for Teams and Leaders," Tammy Redmon has laser vision for seeing breakthrough performance opportunities and the creative ability to transform them into a big win!

Tammy is recognized from Seattle to Shanghai as an author, motivating speaker, facilitator and coach who champions for the power of transformation in leaders, teams, audiences and mastermind groups.

Her vision is to equip leaders and their teams with communication strategies and tools that help every person on the team to better play in the sandbox together.

To find out more about Tammy and her powerful programs, go to www.theteamoptimizer.com or email her today at coach@tammyredmon.com.

Inspiring Team Performance Speaker

Tammy delivers keynotes, coaching and consultations for organizations, teams and leaders who want to bring their teams together to powerfully collaborate, connect and change for the better.

Top 10 Reasons to Hire Tammy:

1. Big team breakthrough success
2. Interactive, hands-on dialogue with participants
3. Insider secrets that can be implemented immediately
4. Ability to pin-point roadblocks to big ideas
5. Relevant, amazing stories
6. Internationally acclaimed leadership team coach
7. Arguably entertaining as a one-of-a-kind speaker
8. Up-to-the-minute lessons from today's leaders
9. Motivating and provocatively inspiring
10. Refreshingly insightful

Online: www.theteamoptimizer.com
Email: coach@tammyredmon.com
Olympia, Washington

"Step up and lead – your team is waiting for you."

Ways to Engage Tammy

Tammy can help your team by delivering powerful talks. Re-frame the way you view your team to create powerful growth, collaboration and profound culture change that contributes to better bottom line with one of these keynote speaking topics:

What do Fortune 100 Leaders Know That You Don't?
Tammy shares nine practices Fortune 100 leaders have mastered to create world-class teams.

3 Reasons Teams Fail and What Every Leader Should Do About It
Tammy unveils the secret weapons your team needs to boost morale, communication and performance.

Get Off the Round-a-Bout and Into the Performance Lane
Revitalize your team with this dynamic personal power speech that gets you to clarity with an action plan for results.

How to Turn Your Problem Employee Around
Tammy helps you identify how much not dealing with an issue really costs you and your team and then how to handle it successfully.

All presentations are fully customizable to meet the specific needs of each unique audience.

Playing in the Sandbox is proudly published by:

Creative Force Press
Guiding Aspiring Authors to Release Their Dream

www.CreativeForcePress.com

Do You Have a Book in You?

Made in the USA
San Bernardino, CA
14 October 2013